# HOLD ON TO ME

A RETRO ROMANTIC COMEDY

CAROLINA CLASSICS
BOOK 2

KAREN GREY

HCB

Published by HOME COOKED BOOKS
A division of Jasper Productions, LLC
www.homecookedbooks.com



ISBN: 978-1-959690-91-7 (paperback)

ISBN: 978-1-7370383-8-2 (ebook)

Subjects: | BISAC: FICTION / Romance / Romantic Comedy. |

FICTION / Romance / Historical / American. |

First edition, November 2022

This is a work of fiction.

Names, characters and events are either a product of the author's imagination [illegible] used fictitiously.



Created with Vellum

## PRAISE FOR YOU GET WHAT YOU GIVE

★★★★★ "Loved the one-night stand plus enemies-to-lovers: 'oops the person I just slept with turns is now my biggest business rival--RIGHT NEXT DOOR.'" - *NYT best-selling author Cathryn Fox*

★★★★★ "Total trip back in time! Especially loved the instant chemistry & the winks to 90's pop culture." USA Today bestselling author Serena Bell

★★★★★ "This enemies-to-lovers, small-town retro romance is bursting with nineties pop-culture fun, deep-seated friendship, and lots of spice!" - *Bookbub review*

★★★★★ "I don't want to wait... to gush about this book! *You Get What You Give* by Karen Grey was a nostalgic romantic throwback to my teenage years that did crazy good things to my heart." - *Goodreads review*

★★★★★ "Smexy tension, banter and wonderful personalities." - *Bookbub review*

★★★★★ "Dust off your MMMbop cassette single and spritz on your Gap Grass fragrance spray we are going back to the 90s... When I say I loved this book I mean I LOVED it!!! It really did remind me of a 90s dramedy where one episode in an ensemble cast focuses on one couple." - *Goodreads review*

★★★★★ "As soon as I finished the prequel to the "Carolina Classics" series, I knew the series and characters were going to be all that and a bag of chips. *You Get What You Give* is a fun and nostalgic story set in the late 1990s that brought me back to my favorite era." - *Bookbub review*

★★★★★ "An absolute must-read... You'll be hooked and like me, chomping at the bit for the next book in the series!" - *Goodreads review*

# CONTENT GUIDANCE

The content notes below are meant to give readers a generalized view of potentially triggering subjects within this novel.

- Use of expletives: frequent but not mean-spirited
- Sex/Nudity: several sex scenes on page
- Violence: boating accident including injuries
- Alcohol use: multiple characters on page
- Description of past trauma: involving familial and sexual relationships of main character
- Abortion: main character (described from past)
- Cheating: main character (described from past)

If you'd like a more detailed list of content warnings (which may include spoilers) they are available at:

https://www.karengrey.com/contentguidance

"You must love in such a way that the person you love feels free."

—Thich Nhat Hanh

"If you find somebody you can love, you can't let that get away."

—*The Wedding Singer*

# CHAPTER 1

"Life is available only in the present moment."

—Thich Nhat Hanh, *Taming the Tiger Within*

SUNDAY, August 16, 1998
Rappahannock River, Virginia

## SULLY

"Mr. Jones, please come out of the cabinet."

My co-captain and I have been living on *Endless Summer* for almost nine months now. I missed my boat almost as much as I missed my friends and family the seven long years I spent in Los Angeles, so when I returned to work on a movie shooting in my hometown this past spring, I pocketed the per diem the show gave me for housing and lived on the sailboat I'd brought back from the dead as a teenager.

"You didn't seem to mind trading an apartment for the salt life when we were in Wallington," I remind him.

Granted, things have been different for the past few weeks. We left the marina behind, traveling up the intracoastal waterway to the Chesapeake Bay. Spending my days sailing and nights anchored in quiet coves has been a dream of mine for years, and despite the drama around my exit from town, the reality has exceeded my expectations. The scenery couldn't be prettier, the weather has been mild for August, and the fishing has been awesome. The past twenty-four hours alone were practically ideal.

Yesterday, after a sweet sail down one river and up the next, we anchored in this little inlet, and I dropped a crab pot in the water before going to bed. By midday today, I'd trapped so many I was able to trade with a family onshore for zucchini and tomatoes.

Meaning, I ate like a king for practically nothing.

Unfortunately, Mr. Jones is less enthusiastic about our current circumstances. I'd venture to say he is not on board with spending a couple months away from civilization.

"Maybe we can rent a slip for a night or two so you could feel solid ground under your feet."

He just growls in response.

"Goddammit, Jonesy!"

I seriously can't believe he's so pissed off that he's hiding in the woodwork. But then I remind myself that I struggle with anger issues too. People think of me as easygoing, but ever since I was little and my brother would tease me to the point that I threw a tantrum, controlling my temper is something I've had to work for.

It helps if I ground myself in sensory experience, so as I lean over the stern to give the dinner dishes an initial rinse, I take the creek's briny scent deep into my nostrils. After swishing the plate, I note the change in the temperature of the air on my hand as I draw it out of the brackish water. When I hear a flutter of wings, I look up to find pair of herons flying to roost in a tree onshore. Before I know it, my frustration with Mr. Jones has floated away like the remains of my dinner.

After I finish cleaning the tiny kitchen, I set up my bed,

planning to take a few moments out on deck before retiring for the night.

When I first tried to meditate with one of the tapes my friend Dani gave me this summer, it was freaking impossible. Tougher than moving across the country without a plan other than following my best friend's lead. More difficult than telling my parents I'd flunked out of college with just a semester left to go.

But on this trip, sitting and counting my breaths just gets easier and easier. Not only have I got an entire sky full of stars to remind me that my troubles don't really mean much in the larger scope of things, but the issues that set me on edge feel far away and unimportant.

Who cares that my parents think I'm a total failure when I'm out here living my dream?

My friends may think I'm an idiot, but my best buddy is still with me, and he'll stop pouting soon.

"Jones?" I still, listening for movement, but get no answer. "All right then. I'll check out the Milky Way by myself, I guess."

After some trial and error, I've gotten pretty good at finding a quiet spot to overnight, where all I hear is the lap of water against the hull, the clink of hardware against the mast, and the chirps of frogs from the shore. But tonight, as I mount the stairs from the cabin to the cockpit, I'm assaulted by sound. Pounding music and the roar of an engine. Thinking it's coming from the land on our starboard side, that's where I look first.

It's only when I look to port that I see the motorboat speeding across the water. I check, and my masthead light is on. Surely the person at the helm will see it. But the boat just keeps getting closer.

Instinctively, I wave my arms and shout, but my voice is drowned by the sounds of the boat, now headed directly at us. Grabbing my safety horn, I blast it a few times before scrambling down the stairs. Shrugging on a life jacket, I look around for something that might keep my little friend afloat.

"Mr. Jones! Seriously, time to come out. I don't have a floatation device to fit a cat, so—"

Before I can finish my sentence, the hull explodes behind me.

# CHAPTER 2

"You look so good with blond hair and black roots it's like not even funny."

*–Romy and Michele's High School Reunion*

BEVERLY HILLS, CA

## *HELEN*

I thought I was ready to face the consequences of my transgression. But when I settle into the chair, Raine's deep groan is laced with anguish.

"I can't believe you'd do this to me. Cheat on me. Again."

"I know. What can I say? I have no self-control."

A palm rises in the space between us. "Talk to the hand, darlin'. Talk to the hand."

I take that hand and give it a tentative squeeze. "Do you forgive me?"

A return squeeze gives me hope, but the disgusted grunt that follows has me on tenterhooks again. I can't live without Raine, but when you're on the road, you have to do what you have to do. "It's just that—"

Raine whips the chair around, and her hands grip its

arms, flanking me. Dark brown irises ringing huge pupils sweep over my face. "Next time you have the urge, call me first. You can't know how much it hurts me when you stray, honey."

I nod, hopeful that we can move on from this. "Believe me, it's worse for me. It just gets to the point when I can't hold back. I'm away from home and you and—"

"And you just go and let any old woman—"

"Well, it was a man this time."

There's a long pause, and I hold my breath as Raine turns away. After what seems like an eon, sure hands snap the shiny black cape into the air. As it settles over me, I can finally breathe again.

"I'll do my best. We're doing color today, too, I assume?"

"If you think."

"Oh, I think."

"Right." I nod, grateful that she seems to have forgiven me. "I've cleared my afternoon for you."

"We're gonna need it, sweet cheeks."

After confirming that my hair is free of product, Raine preps to bleach my roots. Just as she dips a brush into the foul-smelling brew, my cellular phone rings from my bag.

She sighs. "You know I don't like those things in here."

"I do, but I'm crewing up for a new movie job, so I have a lot of calls out."

She points at my briefcase. "You better take it now. Once I start with the bleach, I don't want you putting that thing anywhere near your ear."

"I'll make it quick."

"They say having it by your head all day will give you cancer," she mutters.

I press the button to answer without taking her bait. "Helen O'Neill."

"Hey, Helen. It's Danielle Goodwin returning your call."

The young woman's mellow accent is always a pleasure to

hear, but I cut to the chase. "So, what do you think? Want to come back and work for me?"

"I can't."

"I'll pay you whatever you need."

"I'm sorry, Helen. I'll be forever grateful to you for giving me a start, but I'm juggling four jobs as it is."

"I guess it was too much to expect that you'd be free." Raine's giving me the wrap-it-up finger circle, but I press on. "But if you let those four jobs go and come work for me, you could start moving up the ladder. The minute I get a line producer job, I'd hire you to be my UPM."

"Helen—"

Her tone makes it clear that I'm pushing my luck. "You've said you're not interested, but you're so smart and capable. We need more women like you in the producer pipeline. You could run circles around half the men I've worked for."

"Helen," she repeats, a hint of exasperation coloring her tone.

"All right, all right." I know how to choose my battles as well as change tactics. "So... Any recommendations? What about that friend of yours?"

"Which one?"

"The redhead. The high school teacher. I forget her name."

"Violet?"

"That's it. What about her? I know I pay more than public school."

"She's got her own casting company now."

"Dammit. All the smart women end up being their own bosses."

"If I remember correctly, you're the one who told us to do just that. About fifteen times," she adds, the tease in her voice making me smile despite my disappointment.

"Silly me."

Raine clears her throat dramatically.

"Listen, I've got to go, but if you think of anyone, let me know. And let's get a drink while I'm in town."

After I press the button to hang up, Raine holds out her hand. "Give that thing to me so you're not tempted to answer." She examines the phone before dropping it into a drawer. "I'll admit it's cute. I didn't know they came in colors now."

"That Nokia's the latest fashion accessory, didn't you know?"

She tuts as she begins to apply the bleach. "That's ridiculous."

"I like the bright color because it's easier to find in my purse. And it's so cheap. I can't believe how much I spent on my Motorola—and how often that damn antenna broke off."

"They're all a waste of money, if you ask me."

"It's different for you. You work out of one place. But me, I've got a new office phone with every production. No one would ever be able to find me if I didn't have a cell phone."

"I suppose," she says under her breath as she continues the painstaking process. "So, what's this new movie?"

"It's called *Hacked*." Pretending I'm doing a trailer voice-over, I spit out the logline I've heard so many times I've got it memorized. "'The question isn't why he does it, but how? Based on an unbelievable true story, a prodigy of a programmer run amok bites off more than he can chew when he breaks into the computer of a top security technology expert.'"

"Hm. Sounds… exciting?"

"It's had seven writers. Half the scenes are dudes on computers in basements, and the other half is gobbledygook on computer screens, with a few car chases thrown in for good measure. It'll probably suck."

"But you took the job anyway?"

"If I only worked on good movies, or even decent movies, I'd be sitting at home twiddling my thumbs."

"As long as I've lived in this town, I still don't get how all these bad movies get made," she says as she adjusts the location of a hair clip.

"Somebody somewhere along the line thought every movie had the potential to warrant the investment of millions of dollars. But whether it's too many cooks or trying to recreate last year's hit or an egotistical star's demands, it gets watered down or overloaded to the point that it's ruined."

"And you don't care about that?"

I start to shake my head but firm hands hold it in place. "Those are choices made by the above-the-line folks—the people who make the creative calls and who get a cut of the profits. The director, the big actors, the producers."

"Aren't you a producer?"

"I've been a *line* producer on a few smaller projects, but I'm a unit production manager on this. I report to the LP who reports to the executive producer."

"Talk about too many cooks."

"Exactly. The only creative decisions I make involve how to get the most out of a budget. Like the rest of the crew, I do the best I can with what they give me. Besides, we below-the-line folks get paid even if the film flops."

She snorts as she pores over my scalp, checking her work. "Where is this particular potential flop filming? And for how long? Am I going to have to fly in and rescue this head of hair from your baser impulses?"

"North Carolina. Just for six weeks or so."

"If I remember correctly, Carolina was the place where you got a cut that wasn't half bad."

"High praise."

"That's as good as it gets. Who was that?"

"Let's see. That was a few years ago. It was a girl who was kind of a floater, did hair and makeup. Lily, maybe? No, that's not it. Winnie?"

"I hope you're not like this when you're talking about me."

"Raine, I've known you for more than a decade. I met this girl once. Oh—Whitney, that's right. She was a tiny little thing. Had the sweetest accent and big blue eyes."

This takes us to the subject of the latest Hollywood gossip. Raine's got tons of PR people and agents and managers coming through her salon, so she's got the best dirt. "Speaking of blondes, did you hear Ellen DeGeneres is dating that Anne Heche?"

"The one that's got a haircut like mine?"

"Not as good as yours, but yes."

By the time she's given me the rundown on the other celebrity and industry couples, my hair is slathered.

"All right, you've got about half an hour while this processes. You want a magazine or something?"

"I'd take a coffee, but I've got calls to make."

"You need to learn how to relax."

I stick out my tongue at her. "Phone, please."

"Work, work, work," Raine says disapprovingly, but she digs my phone out of the drawer and hands it over.

I manage to lock in two crew chiefs and I'm about to call the travel coordinator to pass on their contact information when Raine snaps her fingers to get my attention. "Time to wash that out, honey."

After she's done whatever magic she does to tone the color so that I look more like Ellen Barkin and less like Pamela Anderson, she pulls a comb through my hair. "What about the cut? Are we going for Fuck Me or Don't Fuck With Me this time?"

"Can I get a little of both? You know how it is at work. If I don't look and act tough, the men on set will run all over me."

"Mm-hm. I hear you," she croons.

"Buuut I am in a bit of a dry spell on the other front."

"I thought you had a whole lineup of friends you could booty call."

"I did, but they keep pairing off. Every time I get back into town, it's another man down."

"Maybe you need to find one to settle down with."

I wave that suggestion away. "In my experience, the male half of the species is incompatible with monogamy."

She just raises a brow.

I raise a hand in supplication. "Which is fine. As long as everyone is honest about their expectations."

"There is a difference between what you want and what you expect, you know."

I lower my chin and fix her with my most challenging stare. The one I use when a director's claiming I could find money for whatever bright new idea he's had, even though he knows the budget's already set. "I'll settle down when you settle down."

"Girl, you know I like to play the field." She catches my eye in the mirror. "But for different reasons than you."

Raine knows most of my deepest darkest secrets. Hell, she probably knows the secrets of half of the people in this town. She's that good of a hairdresser. And she's right. Whereas she loves the variety—across genders as well as individuals—I'm solidly in the heterosexual monogamy camp.

I let out an uncharacteristic sigh of defeat. "Maybe it's me."

"You can be intimidating."

It's my turn to send a brow raise to the mirror.

"Not to me, silly. Anyhoo, I think I can give you a look that'll do the trick. Sexy when you want, serious when you want. It'll be all about the styling."

When I make a face, she adds, "Don't worry. I know you hate to take time to do your hair." She begins to snip away. "For work, you'll slick it back with gel. That'll tell 'em you mean business."

"Like Gordon Gekko?"

"More like Halle Berry or Neve Campbell. When you want to attract the boys rather than scare 'em off, you go for more texture and volume. Like Winona Ryder."

"I am older than all of these women, you know."

She whaps me lightly on the arm. "Shush. You're as hot as you've ever been. Some of us get better with age."

I have no idea how old Raine is, but her tawny skin is unlined and she's as sassy as she was when we met.

"Raine, is it wrong that my most stable and long-lasting relationship is with my hairdresser?"

"If it is, then there's a lot of wrong in this town. Hell, it could be worse. You could be with someone far less fabulous."

# CHAPTER 3

"People have a hard time letting go of their suffering. Out of a fear of the unknown, they prefer suffering that is familiar."

—Thich Nhat Hanh

SIX WEEKS LATER

Wallington, NC

## SULLY

I'm lying on the couch, staring at whatever movie's on HBO, when my roommate, Dani, walks right in front of the TV and turns it off.

"I was watching that," I protest.

She just crosses her arms over her chest. "What was it?"

I mirror her. "A movie."

Her chin lifts. "What was the name of the movie?"

I mirror her again. "*The... The Broken* something."

It's only then I notice that Dani's got backup: not just my longtime friend Violet and her new boyfriend, Nate, but my used-to-be-best friend, Ford. As in, the guy I haven't really talked to since our fight almost two months ago over a girl that ended up marrying the neighborhood bully from when we were kids.

Go figure.

Violet—never one to mince words or actions—punches me in the arm. "Never bullshit a bullshitter, Sull."

"Ow. You can't punch me. I'm injured," I say, my voice sounding whiny even to me.

"Not in the arm." She notices the dog cuddled next to me on the couch. "Skye. Off."

As Skye slinks off the cushion, Dani says, "You know she's not allowed up there."

"She was comforting me."

Violet sits at the other end of the couch from me, and her ex-enemy / now-boyfriend plops onto the floor at her feet.

"Hey, Sully," Nate says. "Miss you out on the water."

"I miss it too, man." Nate and I met when he first moved to Wallington, and I lent him surfboards because he hadn't brought his own from California.

Both Dani and Ford take a seat, and everyone stares at me.

"What's going on? Is this some kind of intervention or something?"

Violet nods, her face grim. "That's exactly what this is."

"I've been off the drugs since I left the hospital, you know."

"You also haven't left the house," Dani says, ticking a list on her fingers. "You barely get off the couch. You stink. Your muscles are wasting away. You're obviously depressed, and you're not doing anything about any of it."

"Jeez, Dani. Don't hold back or anything."

Nate gives her a look. "That *was* a little harsh."

"I'm with her." Violet sends dagger eyes at Ford and Nate, both of whom shift uncomfortably. "You guys may be weenies, but I care about Sully. Nate, tell him what Veronica said."

Nate clears his throat but when he doesn't speak, Violet pokes him. "Ow. Okay, okay." Turning to me, he asks, "Uh, you know Ronnie?"

"Yeah. Tall blonde that does tricks on a short board?"

He nods. "She was asking about you, and I told her about the accident and your broken tibia. She's a physical therapist and says that you really should be doing exercises every day."

"I'm not cleared for weight-bearing yet," I protest.

He shakes his head. "Apparently, there's a lot you could be doing to strengthen and rebuild all your other muscles. Differing opinions among doctors, I guess, but she said that there's proven benefits, uh, psychologically as well. Especially if you're an athlete and used to using your body a lot."

There's a long pause while I take in the expressions on the faces of my best friends in the world. Well, almost all of my best friends. One is missing. The one that married that jerk Hardy isn't returning anyone's calls.

"Well, *excuse me* if I am a little depressed." Their faces are full of concern, but that somehow makes me angrier, so I begin to tick off a list of my own. "I was the victim of a hit-and-run accident. I barely sleep because I can't get comfortable trying to keep this damn broken leg elevated. The marine police still haven't found the culprits, so I don't know what the hell's up with *Endless Summer*. Even if I did, I can't walk, so I can't work. Meaning, I have no money to even try and fix the boat that I spent hundreds of hours restoring. And if that's not enough, the stack of medical bills on my desk is so high, I can't see around it."

I can't even bring up the thing that I feel the worst about—the loss of Mr. Jones—because I'm afraid I'll lose it, so I leave it at that.

"Sully," Violet says quietly. "You do have every reason to be angry, or sad, or whatever you need to feel. What's scaring us is that you seem numb."

"Yeah, man." Dani rests her elbows on the coffee table and leans closer. "You've always been a pretty chill guy, but this is different. You're like a loggerhead that's pulled into his shell."

"You have health insurance from the union, right?" Nate asks. "Aren't they covering your bills?"

"I do, and I'd really be screwed without it, but still." I shake my head. "Even the co-pay adds up when you're talking a percentage of thousands of dollars. And it can take up to a year to regain full use of my leg, so I don't know if I'll be able to work enough hours to keep the damn insurance."

As they all digest the fact that I do have very good reasons to be both angry and deeply depressed, I wonder if and when Ford will speak. He and Nate both packed up their LA apartments to move to Wallington right around the time my boat got hit, but while Ford's come by, we haven't talked about anything of substance.

When his gaze skitters over me, I catch it with a challenging look. "You have anything to add, Ford?"

He blows out a breath before speaking. "You really want to hear it?"

"Sure. May as well pile on with everybody else."

"We are not piling on, Sully," Violet says. "We're—"

Ford holds up a hand. "Let me say my bit." He shifts in his chair to face me but doesn't continue.

"Spit it out," I say. Possibly growl.

He looks down at his clasped hands. "Maybe because you didn't go to the wedding, it's harder for you to let go."

"Let go?"

"Of Whitney," he says, like I'm the idiot here.

While the faces in this little ad hoc therapy circle are full of what is likely real concern, I'm not ready to admit—even to my closest friends—that it's a hell of a lot harder to be the go-with-the-flow guy when you're drowning.

"But Sully," Violet says, "you are grieving."

"Of course, I am! I mean"—I fling a hand at my useless leg —"look at that thing. It's disgusting."

"Well, that's why we're all here," Dani says.

Ford drops a bulging plastic grocery bag onto the coffee table. "We bring gifts."

# CHAPTER 4

> "Hi, Curly, killed anyone today?"
>
> "Day ain't over yet."
>
> —*City Slickers*

## HELEN

"THIS IS AN EVEN BIGGER FUCKING train wreck than the one you caused yesterday, Michelle!"

When I slam a palm onto the pile of papers on my desk, my assistant flinches. Which pisses me off even more than the giant mess she created.

"Did you even look at that expense report before you faxed it?"

She looks everywhere but at me.

"Did you?"

"I—I, I thought I did. But you made me—"

"I can't *make* you do anything, Michelle. You are an independent autonomous human person. It is your job to proof these reports before they get sent back to LA. But you apparently didn't, and I've got to call a whole bunch of people and explain to them that we aren't five thousand dollars *under* budget, we are five *hundred* dollars over. So they can't spend this supposed windfall on"—I sift through the printouts of emails I received in the past hour—"a trailer upgrade for the co-star that's sleeping with the cinematographer, or the crane rental the director now thinks is essential for the opening shot, or whatever the hell else these idiots want!"

When I shake the printouts in the air between us, she bursts into tears.

"Oh, for fuck's sake. Not the tears."

"I'm sorry," she wails. "You were telling me three things at once, and I got nervous, and I sent the email by accident."

"Why didn't you follow up with another email saying to ignore the first one? Or say something to me about it sometime in the past three hours so I could've gotten in front of the mistake?"

"I was afraid you'd yell at me."

"Well, I'm yelling at you now."

"I know!"

"Michelle"—I begin to pace back and forth in the space between our desks, trying my damnedest to calm down—"if you are too afraid to tell me when you've made a mistake, this isn't going to work. We haven't even started shooting. Things will get even more intense then."

She nods, tears running down her face, her chin wobbling as she tries to hold in future sobs. I'm not going to apologize for yelling at her. She's saddled me with an unplanned set of unpleasant conversations when I should be dealing with a long list of other pre-production tasks. The shooting schedule, the tax credit filing, the union contracts… the list is endless.

I tune out Michelle's sniffles so I can concentrate on fixing her mess. Thankfully, it doesn't take long to find the place where the accountant accidentally added the extra zero. By the time I type up an email with an explanation and a corrected budget report, the crying noise has stopped.

When I look over at my assistant's desk, I discover the

reason why. She's not there. *I* take the time to read over everything one more time before hitting send on the electronic mail and faxing the report.

Everything else seems to be in order, so I uncap a dry-erase marker and face the large whiteboards lining the walls of our office, where I've been gradually filling in schedule details. The unit production manager—the person on location who oversees every penny spent during a movie shoot—would typically keep a separate office from her PA and the set accountants. Partly for confidentiality reasons, partly for intimidation reasons. You don't want to make it too easy for people to come asking for changes to the budget. But I like to keep my assistants close so I can keep tabs on them. Not that the strategy worked with anyone on the list of locals I've hired and fired since arriving in Wallington.

Looking over the calendar, I realize I need the status on the city permits for three location shoots. My assistant was supposed to be running those down, but she hasn't returned from blowing her nose and fixing her makeup. "Michelle! Did we hear back from the city on filming at the waterfront?"

No answer.

"Michelle!"

A chair squeaks in the outer office. A moment later, John Sykes, the second shift accountant, sticks his head in the door.

"She left."

"What do you mean she left? To get coffee?"

"Naw, she quit." His skinny shoulders lift practically to his ears before he drops them again. "Third one this show, O'Neill."

After spending half of yesterday cleaning up after Michelle and the other half looking for her replacement, I'm so far behind today that I don't know which way is up. Principal production starts in less than two weeks, but we don't have a finalized schedule or daily budget, both of which are my primary responsibility. So when my cell phone rings—surprising me because a call getting through is rare in this backwater town—I can't help but bark a "What?" into it instead of a normal human greeting.

"Hey, Helen, it's Dani."

The young woman's self-possessed nature and liquid drawl usually smooth my sharp edges, but right now neither makes a dent in my mad. "Unless you're calling to tell me you're ready to work for me, I don't have time."

"I heard you lost three already."

"How the hell did you hear that? The last one quit less than twenty-four hours ago."

"Bad news travels fast."

"Seriously, Dan, I'm up to my eyeballs in shit here."

"That is why I'm calling. I've got a potential assistant for you."

This news has me collapsing into my chair in relief. "You'd better be serious, girl."

"I am, but he's not your typical candidate."

"Since whatever my typical candidate is hasn't worked out so far, I'm open to suggestions. What's wrong with him? Besides the fact that he's a man."

It's no secret that I hold the fifty percent of the species born with both an X- and a Y-chromosome guilty of being assholes until proven innocent.

"Well, he can't type or take dictation," Dani says. "Basically, he has no office experience."

"What the hell, Dani? I don't have time to fuck around wi—"

"But," she continues, talking over me, "he has seven years on-set experience, working in production sound."

"Why isn't he doing that, then? An office PA gets half the pay of even the third man in that department." My finger trails line items in the half-finished budget on my desk until I find the hourly rate we negotiated for the cable guy on this show. "In fact, it's a little bit less than half. Damn. No benefits, either."

"This guy was in a pretty bad boat accident six weeks ago, and he's still recovering. He's on crutches while his broken leg heals, so there's no way he can haul cables or hold a boom."

"He can't type, he can't walk, and he's a he. Why in the world do you think I should hire him?"

"We used to call him Mr. Serious in college."

"Sounds like a barrel of laughs."

"It's not that he doesn't have a sense of humor. It's that nothing gets to him." She clears her throat pointedly. "*You* won't get to him."

Got to appreciate the balls on this girl. And the perception. "I'm not sure that's possible."

"He needs this, Helen." She groans. "And if I'm being honest here, I need him out of my house."

"Is he your boyfriend?"

"Ew. No way. He's like a brother to me. He was living on his boat, but that got destroyed, so he landed at my place. But he's depressed, and he needs the work."

"You're doing a shit job of selling this dude."

"I have a feeling about this, Helen. I think you'll be good for each other."

"I guess he can't be any worse than the ninnies the local temp agency keeps sending me." I look around the office, at the unpacked boxes, the piles of paperwork to be filed and invoices to be dealt with. "Can he get here today? Wait, can he even drive?"

"It's his left leg that's broken, so yeah. Hang on, I'll just make sure he doesn't have a doctor's appointment or anything."

Her phone clunks onto some hard surface, and I get up to

pace. Whenever possible, I hire women. Or minorities, like John Sykes, who is both gay and black. This business is a men's club where white guys always hire other white guys, which leads to all kinds of shenanigans. Like the producer who hit on the costume designer and then trashed her reputation when she said no. Or the director who had the script supervisor convinced he was in love with her until the show was over and he went back to his wife and kids. Or the actor I respected, until he slept with an underage actress and tried to convince me it wasn't rape.

Not to mention my own ugly experiences.

So, yeah, my trust level with the testosterone-loaded is nil.

I'm about to give up and hang up when Dani returns. "Sorry. He's actually at a doctor's appointment right now, but he left a note saying he'll be back at eleven, so he can be there by midday. Which building are you in?"

I give her the number for our production offices on the Wallington studio lot, thank her, and press the button to end the call. Hands on hips, I forcibly turn my thoughts away from the bad memories, which do not serve in this moment.

If I have to work with a man, maybe I'll be able to shape him into a decent one.

If not, I'll just fire his ass.

# CHAPTER 5

"Sometimes your joy is the source of your smile, but sometimes your smile can be the source of your joy."

—Thich Nhat Hanh

## SULLY

IT'S a good thing I'm not one of those guys who hates to be proven wrong, because every single thing my friends said was right, and every single one of their gifts was something I didn't know I needed.

First off, they very generously paid for a first session with Veronica, and I'm pretty sure she worked with me far longer than she normally would so that I'd have a set of exercises to tide me over while I wait for all the insurance crap to clear.

"Okay," Ronnie says, breaking into my mental wandering. "Last set."

Two months ago, if you'd told me that the hardest workout I'd ever attempt would involve lying on a mat and pointing and flexing my toes, I'd have said you were one fry short of a Happy Meal. I mean, I not only surfed or swam practically every day of my life, I played every sport there was from age five on.

But a long hospital stay plus weeks of lying around on the couch means muscles have atrophied in both legs—the broken and the whole. To make things even more difficult, Ronnie doesn't let me cheat.

"If you use the wrong muscles, you can actually slow your recovery," she explains as the heels of her hands press into my lower back, rolling me more fully onto my right side. "See how your hips are now perpendicular to the ground?"

"Uh-huh," I grunt.

"If you fall out of this position, you won't get the full benefit."

After reminding me to breathe, she counts as I raise my left leg until it's shaking from the effort.

"Okay, good job." She helps me ease onto my back again. "One last set of straight leg raises, and then we'll do some stretches."

She repeats the reminder to breathe as I lift the leg over and over. It takes an enormous amount of mental and physical effort to even get the bum leg off the ground.

After she says I've done enough, she hands me a towel so I can wipe the sweat off my face.

"Tell it to me straight, Ron. Am I going to be able to surf again?" I sit up on my elbows to study the recalcitrant limb. "It's like my damn leg forgot how to do things I don't remember teaching it."

"It ain't gonna be a walk in the park—no pun intended—but yeah, Sull. You're under thirty, you were in fantastic shape before you got hurt, and it seems like your surgeon did a great job."

"I don't know. I hate that my own body feels so foreign."

"The hardest part can be the mental work. You have to figure out how to balance everything you're feeling." She pats me on the shoulder. "Lie down so I can stretch your leg while it's warm. Tell me right away if there's any sharp pain."

As she carefully bends and straightens my left knee, she continues, "It's like you have to go through all the stages of grief. You've suffered a loss—" When I wince, she stills. "That hurt?"

"Not really. There was a weird little click in my knee." What I don't say is that the pain is in my heart. It's embarrassing how much I'm still grieving the loss of my cat and my boat.

"If it just feels weird, that's likely the fascia moving around," she says as she resumes the movement. "That's a good thing. Everything needs to loosen up as well as adapt to the hardware you've got in there."

She shifts position to take my ankle through range of motion exercises, telling me to mirror the movements with my good leg. "Doing that keeps those muscles loose, and helps you remember the stretches so you can do them on your own. I'll send you home with a couple of resistance bands and worksheets."

Once we've completed the exercises, she extends her hand. I take it, and she helps me sit up. "Roll your shoulders and neck to get rid of any residual tension."

I do as instructed while she gathers printouts from a rolling file cart. "Motivation is key. That, and consistency. Results will be slow, which can be frustrating. Patients do best when they process their emotional recovery alongside the physical. You'll have days you don't want to get out of bed. Be compassionate, allow that it's normal to feel defeated, but then you've got to find a reason to take one step. If you can get through this whole regimen every day"—she hands me the stack of paper—"you'll heal faster. But don't give up if that's not possible. Commit to just one thing a day."

We wrap things up, and I thank her again as she escorts me out of the office.

She holds the door open so I can hobble out. "I just want to see you out on your board again, man."

I want that too, but what I *need* is income. Unfortunately, there's nothing I know how to do that doesn't involve being on my feet all day. On a sound crew, I'd have to be able to drag and roll up heavy cables, stand with a boom in my arms, as well as load and unload equipment. If I were the mixer—who mostly sits on his ass all day—I could maybe get away with a bum leg, but I'm nowhere near that level of skill. Ford could probably take it on, but I have no idea what to do with that equipment.

*If you'd only apply yourself, you'd live up to your potential.* Words aimed at me by all my teachers, guidance counselors, and both of my parents.

My answer? I apply myself when I care. I just never cared about anything other than being on the water. Whether it was a Boogie board or surfboard or kayak or sailboat, that was all I ever cared about.

My priorities haven't changed, but I have no idea how I can use what I know to support myself, let alone afford the activities I love, even if I were healthy enough to do them.

As my frustration builds, I remember something Ronnie said about dealing with the difficulties of recovery: *commit to just one thing a day*. On the boat, I started listening to these cassette tapes that had a similar message. Ironically, they were about walking meditation, which I couldn't do on the boat, and I sure can't do now. But the dude who recorded them, Thich Nhat Hanh, had a lot of wise things to say. Like, when trying to calm negative energy, you can't fight it. Instead, you smile at it and then invite something in to replace it.

Like doing a workout. Or listening to music. So, after doing my best to mindfully crutch my way across the parking lot, I grab the CD mix Ford made for me—just one of the gifts dumped out of that plastic bag the other day—planning to trade negative thoughts for some Smashing Pumpkins and Pearl Jam.

My head's still bobbing along with the echoes of Dinosaur Jr.'s "Feel the Pain" as I limp through the front door of Dani's house, but the music fades when I see the look on her face. "You look like the cat that ate the canary."

"You look like Ronnie worked your ass off."

"You got that right." Setting one crutch against the kitchen counter, I grab a glass from the counter, fill it with water, and chug it down. "But it was good. I appreciate you guys paying for that. I think the exercises are just what I need to get me through until my appointment with the local orthopedist."

"I'm glad." She's still got the funny look on her face.

"Spit it out, whatever it is."

She leans against the counter and folds her arms across her chest. "Well, I have another surprise for you."

"A good surprise or a bad surprise?"

She tips her head to the side. "I think it's an excellent surprise. But I'm not sure you're going to agree."

I maneuver over to a barstool. "Just tell me already."

After she explains, all I can think to say is, "Isn't she the lady you were terrified of?"

"Only at first. She is a caution. But she was also the best boss I ever had. Just don't let her rattle you." Dani shakes her head with a laugh. "What am I saying? Nothing rattles you."

I clamp my mouth shut before the truth escapes. That *everything* rattles me these days. I never used to worry about anything. Now I have nightmares and so many worries I can't keep track of them.

Not to mention the guilt that has kept me pinned to the couch.

Or the regret.

Or the anger.

Thing is, I can't go back and make different choices. But I can accept what is and move on.

Whitney's married.

*Endless Summer* is done for.

And Mr. Jones is probably dead.

But I will surf again, I will get out of debt, and I will be independent again.

Maybe going head-to-head with a ballbuster is exactly what I need to get me there.

Dani convinces me to take the interview for the PA job before telling me that I have to be there by noon. The studios aren't far from the bungalow she inherited from her aunt, but taking a shower is no easy task these days. I don't have to worry about getting the incision wet anymore, but it's hard for me to get in and out of the tub.

Still, my gut tells me that I need this, so I get through it as quick as I can, avoiding the sight of my wasted frame in the mirror. My shoulders and arms have a little more definition from using the crutches, but both of my legs are pitiful excuses of what they used to be.

As far as this interview goes, though, the state of my physique is the least of my worries. I've never worked in an office before. Besides recording sound for TV and movies, I've done odd jobs at a marina, parked cars, and worked the line in a hotel kitchen. Reading, writing and 'rithmatic were never my strong suits in school, and I'm pretty sure all those things are important if you're a producer. Or her assistant.

Before I dive into yet another depression spiral, I get myself to my car and switch out the rock for *The Art of Mindful Living*. By the time I've parked, I'm hanging on to what Mr. Hanh said about taking care of the future by taking care of the present.

One breath at a time. One hitching step at a time.

I know the Wallington sound stages like the back of my

hand, but the only time I ever entered the production offices was when something was wrong with my paycheck. The directory includes a map of the warren-like building, but it takes me a few moments to figure out how to get from the map's *You Are Here* to the offices for the film *Hacked*. Just as I turn to head in that direction, the doors at the end of the hallway fly open, and the most gorgeous woman I've ever seen appears.

With that kind of presence, she's got to be the star of some movie shooting in town. Gesturing animatedly, she talks a mile a minute to the two people following in her wake. Short hair the color of corn silk arches above wide-set green eyes. An expressive mouth is lined in a sexy mocha tint I want to taste. Her ivory skin tone tells me she's not a sun-worshipping local.

Slack-jawed, probably drooling all over the floor, I catch a tantalizing whiff of sage and citrus as she storms by, passing me without a nod or a smile. Definitely not a southern woman, then. They can't cross paths with anyone without a wave or a "Hey, how're you?"

"Wait."

At the command, we all freeze, her posse parts, and the woman points at me. "You're on crutches," she says, like she's accusing me of a major transgression.

"I-I am."

"You're Dani's friend."

"Y-yeah." For some reason, my brain is back to stuttering like it did right after the accident.

"You're late." With that, the one-person hurricane resumes its path, but when she reaches a doorway, she pauses to glance back at me.

"What the hell are you waiting for?"

Hell of a question.

One for which I am not sure I have an answer.

# CHAPTER 6

"What I am concerned with is detail. I asked you go get me a packet of Sweet-N-Low. You bring me back Equal. That isn't what I asked for. That isn't what I wanted. That isn't what I needed and that shit isn't going to work around here."

—*Swimming With Sharks*

## HELEN

WHEN WE PASSED the hunkalicious giant in the hall, every cell in my body went on alert. From dark curls framing a face chiseled to perfection to broad shoulders looking like they bear the weight of the world, to a scowl he's not even trying to suppress, this guy is all kinds of catnip for me.

However, I've learned the hard way that mixing business with pleasure does not make for happy endings, so once I realize he's my potential new assistant, I use the trip back to my office to pack all those feelings away.

By the time he's swinging long legs through the doorway, I've got those pesky primal urges under control. Since it'll be awkward for him to shake my hand with both of his occupied by crutches, I pull out a chair, give him a curt nod, and cross to the other side of my desk. "You must be Sully. I'm Helen O'Neill."

"I figured. Nice to meet you."

*That lilting accent layered over a rich baritone… This could be dangerous, O'Neill.*

"Everything all right?" he asks.

Schooling my expression to a polite smile, I gesture at the piles of boxes behind him. "I was just thinking that you may have a difficult time with some of the necessary duties. Because of your injury. Usually, I'd have my assistant unpack these—"

"I'll figure it out." He turns briefly to examine the mess. "Actually, would you mind if I use a couple of those boxes to elevate this thing for the interview? If I don't, it'll swell up."

"Whatever you need," I say, even as my brain supplies ideas for other things that might swell up and how he might satisfy other needs.

He nods before effortlessly dragging a box closer to him. "Thank you, Mrs. O'Neill."

"Mrs. O'Neill was my mother. You can call me Helen, or O'Neill. Got it?"

"Got it, O'Neill."

As he gets settled, I straighten the piles on my desk. "I don't typically do an interview since I don't bring anyone in unless they come highly recommended. Instead, I have the candidate do a trial day or two. That includes shadowing me, so let's talk about that bum leg of yours."

"Well, my boat was anchored up in the Chesapeake Bay, and this other boat slam—"

I cut him off with a hand in the air. "I don't need to hear the details of your accident."

"Wow." He coughs out a half-laugh. "That's pretty harsh."

"I'm sorry that whatever happened happened, but what's relevant here is: are you sure you're ready to go back to work?"

He takes a beat before speaking. "My doctor doesn't want me putting weight on the injured leg yet or standing for long periods—necessary in my previous positions—but I am cleared to work otherwise."

"I need to know that you can keep up with me."

"Depends on how fast you walk, I suppose."

I shoot him a glare to make it clear I don't have time for making fun. "Not physically. Obviously, I'm not enrolling you in a sack race. I mean task-wise. If your leg isn't a limitation to you getting the work done, if you can pick everything up in a couple of days, you'll stay."

"Sounds doable."

"It's not easy. There is a lot of information to manage, and it comes from all directions all day long. And the *day* is long because we're dealing with crews on this coast as well as producers and editors who are three hours behind us."

He turns the full force of his gaze on me again. "I'm pretty sure I can handle that, but I can't get you coffee."

"Did I ask you to get me coffee?"

"I just assume that's what assistants do."

I wave a finger back and forth. "Never assume. If you don't know, ask. The thing I hate most is when people are afraid to ask me shit. Even if I snap at you because I'm in the middle of something, I need you to ask instead of assuming you know what to do and then doing the wrong thing. I don't bite, but I do bark. Got it?"

"Got it."

"People call me a bitch. I don't care about that. What I care about is honesty. I need to know everything that's going on because inevitably what someone's hiding is going to come back and bite us all in the ass."

"Understood." He shifts in the chair and his biceps bulge, the hairs on his forearm glinting gold even in the shitty fluorescent light. "I'll be honest, then. I have no idea what a UPM does, let alone a UPM's assistant."

Instead of asking why the hell he's applying for the job, since it's likely Dani strong-armed him into it, I give him the rundown. "The UPM manages all cost-related decisions, and I'm the eyes and ears on the ground for the producers back in LA. Along with the production coordinator, it's my responsibility to oversee all physical aspects of the production. I hire the crew, deal with housing and transpo, write and rewrite the schedule, and liaise with all local authorities, like the police and city permit offices. Most important, though, I hold the purse strings. It's my job to make sure that the fifteen million and change of this show's budget is spent wisely."

He nods slowly, his expression difficult to read. "And your assistant?"

"You keep track of the paper trail." I gesture to the outer office. "Dee and John handle the accounts payable and payroll. With them, you'll generate a daily report of hot costs—"

"Hot costs?"

"That's the comparison of budgeted to actual costs. We need to know how much we're over or under each day and where those disparities are happening so we can adjust."

I get up to pace. "There're also incoming faxes and emails. First task of the morning is to go through what came in while we slept. Everything gets copied, sorted, and prioritized. Invoices and receipts go to accounting. New expenditure requests—of which there will be a lot—go directly to me. You'll work with the production coordinator's assistant to manage script changes. You'll have to memorize the WGA page colors for revisions. Blue for V2, Pink for V3, Yellow f—"

"For version four," he cuts in. "Green for five, yada yada yada. I know them from working in sound."

"Right. Good."

"Will I also make the script half-sheets for the crew every day?"

"The coordinator's PA does that. Our job is to identify

what those changes are going to mean for the budget and schedule. Like if they decide not to use the Jaguar one of the leads drives in a certain scene, I need to know so that we can cancel that very expensive rental for the day. Capiche?"

As I continue with the litany of duties my assistant needs to keep up with, it occurs to me that while he's sitting there looking gorgeous, he's not writing anything down. "I really don't have time to go over this more than once. Are you going to take notes?"

"Do you want me to take notes?"

"Are you going to remember everything without writing it down?"

"Yes, but if you'd feel better if I take notes, then I will."

I side eye the guy as I drop into my chair. "Are you fucking with me?"

His brow furrows slightly. "No. You know the job; I don't. So, I should do it the way you tell me to. I heard you say that I should ask questions when I need to and not be afraid of your bark…"

He goes on to list every single thing I've said so far, verbatim, until I hold up a hand to stop him. "Okay, Mr. Photographic Memory, I get the point."

"I don't have a photogr—"

"Whatever."

"Do I make you uncomfortable?" he asks.

I pick up a pen and tap a rhythm on the desk as I consider the question. He does make me edgy but not in a way that I'll ever admit. "Why do you ask?"

"I'm a big guy." *He* looks uncomfortable as he scans the crowded office. "And this is a small space. In the sound department, I was told early on that I always had to have another woman present when I put a wire on an actress in her trailer. Because of my size and gender."

"Oh. No. I'm not worried about your size." My attention caught by the very large foot resting on the stack of boxes, all

I can think about is that old saw about the correlation between shoe size and penis size.

*Totally inappropriate, Helen.* "Yes, well, that would be inappropriate—I mean, totally *appropriate* for you to have another woman present in that situation. But we're fine here. Totally fine."

He nods, looking less than convinced by my rambling answer. "Okay, what else do you need me to do?"

Filing what I'd *like* to do with him in a far back corner of my brain, I return to the tasks at hand. "I'm guessing you don't need a tour of the studios since you've worked here before?"

"Correct."

"But I do think we'll need to get you a golf cart. Dani said you can drive, but you can't type."

"It'll be hunt and peck. I might need an introduction to your computer. It's been a while since I used one."

"I can get someone to do that. Meanwhile, you have forms to fill out."

"I'm a damn expert at that."

This sudden shift into a caustic tone knocks a cough of surprise out of me.

"Sorry," he continues. "It's just that since the accident, I've filled out more forms and signed my life away more times than you could imagine."

"That sucks, but you'll have to do it again." I pull the necessary forms from a box next to my desk. "Get going on these. When you're done, your first official duty will be to file them. Along with the others in that basket. Cabinets are labeled, the system should be obvious."

He nods.

I hope I'm a bigger person than the piece-of-shit producer who hired me when I was just a kid, but the words that come out of my mouth next make me wonder if that's true. "If this injury is going to be a pain in the ass for me, then you'd better be worth it."

His smile in response is wicked. "I will make sure that my injury is only a pain in my ass, O'Neill."

Unfortunately, his tone belies his words. But I can't dwell on that. I've got work to do. Usually, an assistant's first day is all about whether they can keep up with me without falling apart.

I have a sinking feeling that this one is going to be the opposite.

# CHAPTER 7

> "When another person makes you suffer, it is because he suffers deeply within himself, and his suffering is spilling over. He does not need punishment; he needs help. That's the message he is sending."
>
> —Thich Nhat Hanh

## SULLY

SINCE I'D EXPECTED a half hour or so spent in an interview rather than hours spent on a first day of work, I didn't eat lunch before I drove over. I'm also supposed to keep up my protein and calcium intake, so when my stomach grumbles the third time in a row, I cry uncle.

"Sorry, Helen, but I need to eat. Healing bones and all that."

Helen looks at her watch. "Get out of here, then. The show in Stage 4 is probably breaking for lunch right now. You can get something there."

"Do you want anything?"

"I'm fine."

I haven't seen the woman take in anything but coffee all day, but my mom usually only eats one meal a day. Maybe she's like that. Not that there's anything mom-like about O'Neill. Which is what I have to call her in my head. Somehow, thinking of her as Helen is much more dangerous. No matter how much I'd like to, hitting on the boss seems like a bad idea.

Not that she seems interested.

"Are you going or what?" she barks in that city accent of hers.

"I'm going."

As I'm crossing the threshold, she asks, "Do you have a pager?"

It's too much trouble to turn my entire body around, so I just turn my head. "I do, somewhere. But I'm just going across the lot."

"Yeah. You're right. Fine." She does that erasing thing in the air, like she just wants me to disappear. So I do.

Working for this woman is going to drive me crazy in more ways than one, but there's something telling me that I need this. It's not just the money. Every once in a while, I get this gut feeling that I need to learn something from someone, and I'm getting it loud and clear with Helen.

O'Neill, I mean.

Just as I'm wondering what I can do to make myself a more appealing candidate for the job, a familiar voice calls out my name.

"Sully? What are you doing here?"

My friend Violet steps into the sunlight. Her colorful skirt flaps around her legs as she jogs to catch up with me.

I point to the catering tent in the lane ahead of us. "Getting some lunch."

"You're working?" She tips her head to the side. "I didn't think you could."

"Not in sound, but Dani got me a chance at a PA job. UPM's assistant on this movie that starts up in a week or so."

Violet makes a face. "Is it even worth it? Will you make more than you would in unemployment?"

"It's crap compared to the sound utility guy rate, but I, uh, forgot to file for unemployment."

"What about disability?"

I shrug. "I don't think I qualify for that."

"Well, we should look into it." Violet is a casting director, which gives her an excuse to be all up in everyone's business. "What's the show, and who would you work for?"

"*Hacked.* Helen O'Neill."

"Oh," she says, looking like somebody licked the red off her lollipop.

"What's wrong?"

"She kind of has a… a reputation."

"Yeah, she told me people call her a bitch."

"She did? Dang."

"Said she doesn't care."

"Good for her. Wish I could be more like that."

When we arrive at the catering truck, without even asking, Vi puts two plates and two sets of silverware on her cafeteria tray. I hadn't thought about the fact that on crutches I can't juggle a tray on my own. After we go through the line and get settled at a table, I ask, "Where's Nate?"

"He has a lunch meeting. Fundraising something or other for Surfrider."

"That's cool he's doing that." I shovel meatloaf into my mouth, wishing I hadn't asked. I love that Nate's helping to save the oceans, but I hate that I can't be a part of that community right now.

Vi pats me on the arm. "You'll be back in the water before you know it, Sull."

I just nod and change the subject. As we chat, I'm grateful that she avoids other ugly topics like surfing and boating and Whitney, but she does surprise me with gossip about Ford.

"Apparently, he's seeing a stand-in on *Lawson's Reach*."

"Yeah?" I don't mention the fact that Ford hasn't talked to me about it, but I also know I don't need to ask for more intel, because Violet won't be able to stop herself from telling all.

"She *just* graduated from the School of the Arts up in Winston-Salem."

"The high school? How old is she?"

"From the BFA program." She leans closer. "But still, she's only twenty-two."

"Cradle-robber."

She shakes her head. "She is awful cute, but…"

*She looks like Whit?* almost escapes from my mouth, but I catch myself and say instead, "Well, good for him."

"I'm not so sure it is good for him. She's the fourth girl he's gone out with since he got back in town."

"Since Whitney's wedding, you mean?"

"You said it, not me." She scoops up a forkful of salad. "Have you talked to him?"

I know what she means, but I dodge it anyway. "You were there the other night when he was over."

"Yeah, and I noticed the fact that you barely said a word to each other." She sits back in her chair. "What happened to you two?"

Pushing the meatloaf that no longer looks appetizing around my plate, I almost answer, *I don't know.* But that would be a lie.

She doesn't wait for me to spit it out. Violet never does. "I mean, I get it. You're both in love with the same girl. But isn't your lifelong friendship more important?"

We've all been friends since preschool, but it hasn't always been sunshine and roses for Ford and me. The thing is, it took me a while to figure that out, so maybe Violet hasn't either. "It's kind of hard when your best friend is perfect, you know."

This shuts her up. For a second. "What are you talking about?"

I stab my fork into the mound of mashed potatoes on my plate and then watch as it slowly tips to the side. "Just like with my brother, all I ever heard was 'Why can't you be more like Ford?' He and Ken got good grades, got all the way through Eagle Scouts, were the presidents of every damn club they joined. Whereas I got Cs and Ds and flunked out of college with one semester to go."

For once, Violet has nothing to say. Instead, she buses our dishes. She doesn't even press for more as we walk back across the lot. I actually feel a little bit better having unloaded, but I'm still a little worried about the fact that I so obviously lack the necessary skills that I might lose this chance at a job I can do while my leg heals. But when Violet stops in front of her building and wishes me luck, it suddenly occurs to me that she has a *lot* of experience working in offices.

"Yeah, so, Vi, I've kind of got this job on a trial basis. Any tips for me? Like, how do you stay organized?"

"You're really going for it?" she asks, her tone laced with skepticism.

Whether she thinks I'm unsuited for the job or that it's not worth my time, it doesn't matter. "Dude. Working as a PA may be going backwards, but it's the only job I've got right now. I could use all the help I can get to hold on to it."

She blows out a breath, like she's considering how to even start. "Well, filing is key. To-do lists are key."

I can't help the groan that comes out of my mouth as I picture the piles of paperwork and row of filing cabinets in the *Hacked* offices. "Ugh. Feels like school."

She faces me, hands on hips. "Do you leave your surfboards in a pile all higgledy-piggledy?"

I take a half step back, affronted. "Of course not. One, they'd get scratched. Two, it'd take forever to find the one I want."

Brows up, she nods slowly, like, *No shit, Sherlock,* and then crosses her arms. "So how do you avoid that?"

Thinking that the high school kids must've totally loved *and* hated having her as a teacher, I picture the shed in my mind. The one I haven't been to in what feels like years even though it's only been a couple of months. "I arrange them according to size and type."

She shrugs. "That's filing."

"What do you mean?"

"It's just putting things in order. Only difference is, when you file papers, you use the alphabet. Unless she's got some other system."

"I don't know… that seems—"

"What about the sailboat?"

"What about it?"

"You always bragged how you managed to pack tons of stuff in its tiny cabin."

"First of all, the boat's a her," I correct. "But, yeah, I had to make sure to stow my supplies and tools and stuff so things wouldn't go flying when you tack or hit some weather."

"Pfft." She waves a hand in the air. "Same with an office."

"What?" I snort out a laugh. "In case of a hurricane?"

"No, dummy. You keep your belongings"—she makes air quotes—"'shipshape' so you know how to find them when you need them. Like, I hate spending extra time looking for a stapler because *someone* didn't put it back in its place in the drawer. If only Nate would ask for organizational guidance. Come on, I'll show you." She gestures for me to follow her inside the building that houses Carolina Casting. Or Casting Carolina. I can never remember which name they ended up with.

"How long do you think it'll take?" I ask, wondering how long I'm allowed to take for lunch.

"I'll just give you a quick tour of my drawers—"

"Your drawers!" I say with a *Beavis and Butthead* snicker.

She groans. "Oh my god, don't be such a boy."

"Can't help it. 'I yam what I yam.'"

"You better not act that way around Helen O'Neill."

"You're right. I need to practice being more professional. Things are probably a bit looser on set than in the offices."

"It's a different world when you're with the suits, that's for sure." She unlocks her office door. "I've got some ideas that'll knock her socks off."

Stowing the thought of what I'd really like to knock off of my new boss, I dutifully follow Violet inside.

After working for her for just a few days, I've learned that Helen—I mean, O'Neill—is a bit of a control freak. Actually, she's a total control freak. I can imagine how someone working for her might've made extra mistakes just because she's so in your face.

Thing is, dealing with people who are prepared to be disappointed in me is something I'm totally used to. At some point—junior high, I think it was—I figured out that I was never going to measure up to my older brother's accomplishments. Teachers got exasperated when I refused to do anything I wasn't interested in, but to me, it wasn't worth beating myself up when I found a subject both boring and mystifying. So I just stopped giving a shit. It didn't make my parents, or really anyone else except me, happy, but I sure was less tense.

When O'Neill spends half an hour explaining how to make copies, I nod and smile and then just do it the way that makes sense to me. When she hovers over me, hissing instructions in my ear when I'm talking to the AD or a city official on the phone, I just ignore her. When she yells because she can't find something, I calmly find what's missing and place it in front of her.

Half the time she blows her top, she's just letting off steam. I get it. She's in charge of more money than I'll ever have in a bank account. That's probably stressful.

But why should I let it get to me?

The only real issue I'm having has to do with being on crutches. I figured this'd literally be a desk job, but only half my time is butt in chair. There's a lot of back and forth to the copy room, other offices. Even getting something from my desk to the file cabinets is a challenge because I can't carry anything I can't jam into the space between my palm and the hand rest. I'm not going to give up, though.

Instead, I improvise. After I Xerox the latest so-called final shooting schedule—there's been a new "final" schedule every day this week—I decide to use a rolling chair to transport the pile of carefully collated copies back to the office. All I have to do is move slowly and smoothly enough that they won't fall off. It works like a charm—for about ten feet. Then, almost in slow motion, my beautiful stack turns into the Leaning Tower of Pisa. Before I can drop a crutch to stop it, the last hour's work is spread all over the hall.

"Son of a bitch! Argh!"

The prop master sticks his head out of the nearest open door. "You okay?"

"Yeah, sorry for disturbing you. I'm fine, but my copies bit it." I gesture at the rolling chair. "Guess that was a stupid idea."

The guy scratches his soul patch as he takes in the scene. "How come you didn't sit in the chair and put the copies on your lap?"

"I tried that, but I couldn't get down the hall with only one good leg. I kept going in circles."

He nods slowly, then snaps his fingers. "Aha! I've got a wheelchair in storage. It even has little pockets on the sides you can stick stuff in."

"Seriously? That would be awesome."

He not only helps me clean up the mess, but less than an hour, later he shows up with the promised wheelchair.

Four days into this job, I'm cruising. Literally and figuratively. Not only can I get stuff where it needs to go, but the wheelchair lets me elevate my leg easily when I'm sitting for any length of time. I'm in a better frame of mind, and it turns out that office work is kind of fun. I wouldn't want to do a regular nine-to-five job, but I'm enjoying figuring out systems for all the tasks that need doing.

I even have a to-do list.

I started keeping it because it made O'Neill so nervous that I didn't. But now—and I'll never admit it to my mom or any of the teachers that suggested I use the planner they gave us in high school—I actually enjoy ticking its boxes.

Which makes me wonder: how many useful tools did I reject simply because my brother or Ford or Violet used them? Like highlighting your notes with different colors to help you… I don't even know what, because it seemed dumb, and who even took notes anyway?

Writing due dates in a calendar so you wouldn't forget about an assignment until the night before? *Lame.*

Keeping a list of things that need to get done? I always thought: if it's really important, I'll remember it.

And that's the thing. When it's important to *me,* I remember it. But what if it's important to the people around me? Maybe it's time for me to start taking them into account too. Not to prove that I'm worthy or good enough, but just out of kindness and compassion.

From the tapes I've been listening to on the way to and from work, it seems like I've been living my whole life in reaction to what I think other people want me to do. As in, reacting negatively.

Just like I have to re-teach some of my muscles, I might have to re-think some of my assumptions. Why not use tools like to-do lists if they're helpful? I wouldn't try to build something with just a hammer and nails when there's a power saw and an electric drill in the shop. Sometimes one tool is best for the job; sometimes you need another.

By Friday afternoon, I am not only keeping a color-coded to-do list, but I have also checked each and every box. O'Neill's office is free of shipping boxes, and all the paperwork is filed. The fax machine is empty, and mailboxes are full. Since the boss is out meeting with the police department about street closings, and John Sykes is all caught up on his accounting duties, we decide to engage in a little desktop football while we wait for Helen to return.

Sykes is from Detroit, so his team is the Lions. North Carolina didn't have a team growing up but got the Panthers while I was away in California, so that's mine. Logic dictates that when one of us scores, we roar.

I'm mid-howl when John's eyes go wide like there's an actual feline predator behind me. After choking back the sound, I turn to find O'Neill staring at us like we've lost our minds.

"Heh-hey, boss," John says. "We were uh, just taking a break."

"How nice for you," she says. Then, arms crossed over her chest, she rattles off a series of questions. I can tell that she really wants to catch me out, and that it pisses her off every time I say "Done."

Because it means she has no real reason to yell at me.

# CHAPTER 8

"That'll do, pig.... That'll do."

—*Babe*

## HELEN

SULLY IS damn good at this job for a person who has none of the skills I deemed necessary for the job. Touch typing, a familiarity with office computer software... hell, I used to think being a steno was vital.

Of course, that was back in the late eighties when an office PA was more likely to use a Selectric than a laptop, and an executive wouldn't be caught dead typing his own letters.

But now, it's easier for me to tap out my own electronic mail messages and memos. Meanwhile, anything I tell him to do just gets done. If he has a problem, he fixes it. I've never had an assistant who was such a self-starter. Except Dani.

Not that he ever does anything exactly the way I tell him to. He always has to change things up somehow. I can't tell if he does it to push my buttons, or if he's just a rebel, but since the results are what I expect, I do my best to not get all bent out of shape about it.

The only real problem I'm having with Mr. Calloway has to do with sharing my office. Not only does the man not require supervision, but he's a distraction. I've been telling myself for the past few days that it's his size and the space he and his crutches—and now, his wheelchair—consume. But it's more than that.

Just existing in the same small space with him stirs up desires I can't act on. This country may have had a sexual revolution, but a woman who sleeps around still loses the respect of her male colleagues. I need every inch of authority I can muster to do this job, otherwise the director and cinematographer will go over my head when I tell them no, like kids going to their dad when mom says no. On top of all that, I refuse to get involved with someone over whom I have power. Sully may outweigh me, but I'm the one who signs his paycheck.

Even if I avoid acting on them, the fantasies he inspires take up too much brain space. When his scent wafts across the room, the briny, musky cocktail enters my nose, deactivates my frontal lobe, and I'm suddenly stupid with lust. The wheelchair squeaks, and I'm neck deep in an imagined scenario involving the headboard to my bed making the exact same noise.

Over and over again.

I shelve that image, only to have my eye caught by his reach to open a file drawer. Muscles that seem to gain definition by the day ripple across shoulders, back, and arms. My hands twitch with the need to dive under the fabric of the production logo T-shirt of the day and memorize the landscape of what's underneath.

It's just so much temptation right under my nose. I don't want to fire him. He needs the job, and I need a competent assistant. But he's got to move to the outer office if I'm ever going to get anything done.

⛵

## SULLY

The next day, I arrive to find my desk in the larger front room instead of inside O'Neill's office. Not sure whether it's punishment or banishment, I stow my backpack, get my butt into the wheelchair, and lean my crutches against the wall.

I'm booting up the computer and leafing through faxes when Helen yells from inside her office. "Calloway?"

Without thinking, I just yell back "O'Neill?" echoing her tone. Sassy, but if she moved me out here, she's got to realize that she can't get to me as fast as if I were in the room with her.

She appears in the doorway, a frown on her face. "Well, this is going to be a pain in the ass."

"Then why'd you move me out here?" There's something about her direct attack that just cracks me up. This woman has made me laugh more in the past week than I have in the past two months. I guess I could see how some people might find it unnerving, but I think she's hilarious.

"I noticed you were having a hard time getting in and out of this doorway in the wheelchair," she says, gesturing at my desk. "Plus, sitting there you can be like a... what do you call it?"

"Receptionist?"

"Eh, more like a bouncer. Keep out the riffraff."

"You get a lot of lowlifes in here?"

"No, ya big lug. It's just another level of triage. They have to get by you to get to me."

"You're the boss." I tip my chin past her, toward the filing cabinets lining the walls of her office. "You gonna move those out here too?"

She studies them, her mouth pursed. Her lipstick, always

dark, has a more purplish tone to it today. A pair of fat plums, warm from the sun.

"Calloway. Eyes up here."

My face hot, I force my gaze away from lips begging for a kiss. "Sorry. Zoned out for a minute."

"I *said*, I'm still thinking about the filing cabinets, but right now I need you to get on the script changes. I got electronic mail from one of the producers with the news that they've brought in another writer—bringing our grand total up to eight—to, I quote, punch up the dialogue, unquote. So there are going to be a lot of new pages. Why they think it's okay to pull this kind of shit just days before we start shooting..." she mutters, heading back in her office. Once inside, she yells, "Don't hang around listening to me complain. You need to get to Glenda's office to pick up those pages."

"Yup. On it, boss."

## HELEN

Moving Sully out of my office solved one problem but created another. Now, he can't just look up and answer when I have a question. He also can't jump up and come to the doorway when I call. At first, we just yelled back and forth, but then the accountants complained that we were disturbing their concentration.

But that's why phones were invented.

Now, I know he knows that the FedEx pickup time is 4:45 p.m. There's a poster with the time right by the door. But it's especially important that the package he's putting together goes out today. I've spent the entire day adjusting the schedule with the first AD and then moving shit around in the budget to accommodate the new scenes. Everything except the extra car chase, that is. The line producer backed me up and told the director himself: if they want to add another chase, it needs to be on foot because we can't afford the added costs of car rentals, insurance, and permitting.

The rest of the crew and cast arrive in days, and I would really like to get the new schedule and budget approved before that invasion. Therefore, it's vital that the west coast powers that be to get the package tomorrow.

So I buzz him again.

"Calloway, just making sure you know you've got to get that report to me by four thirty at the latest. Because the FedEx pickup time is—"

"Four forty-five. I know, O'Neill."

And then he hangs up on me.

I want to throw a hissy fit, but instead I take a deep breath. I already gave him a detailed list of what needs to be included. If I can trust him to follow it, that frees me up to comb through the quotes from the two local crane rental companies. It would be a much more efficient use of my time, but it's hard to concentrate when I can't see him actually doing the work.

I'll just buzz him one more time to make sure he understands how important meeting this deadline is.

He doesn't answer, so I get up to see what's going on, but by the time I get to the doorway, he's hopped halfway around his desk.

"Goddammit, O'Neill," he growls, expression and tone thunderous. "You will get this report when I am done with it. You interrupting me to bug me about it is slowing me down, not making me work faster. So leave me the fuck alone!"

My gaze skitters over to the audience for this scene: the two accountants in the room. Only John has the courage to meet my eyes, and he gives me a shrug that says *You know he's right.*

I turn to face Sully. "I'm sorry. You're right."

"Get out of my face then."

There was a time when I would've fired anyone who talked back to me like Sully just did. But I've got to respect the fact that this man cares enough about the actual work to tell it to me straight.

"Right. I will be in my office when it's ready."

## SULLY

After Helen quietly closes the door behind her, I hop back around the desk and lower my ass into my chair.

I feel guilty for about three seconds, but it's the same regret I'd feel for killing a particularly persistent mosquito. Helen being on me like white on rice about this report is simply not useful.

In fact, now that she's stopped buzzing that damn intercom every five minutes, I get the stack of paper hole-punched, bound, and on her desk *before* the deadline.

After the FedEx guy comes and goes, though, all that righteous anger dissipates.

I don't like being ruled by my temper. Even with grief as an excuse, I need to shift that energy. Otherwise, it'll continue to swamp me or make me bitter or fester so that I keep blowing up.

What I need to do is funnel it into repairing my body. And my head.

## HELEN

Five minutes after the FedEx pickup, Sully hops into my doorway, this time with a sheepish look on his face. "I apologize for losing my temper."

I wave it off, hoping that'll shoo away some of the feelings I've developed for this man. "Shit happens. Just don't make a habit of it."

"I don't. I mean, I won't."

"People blow up. Tensions get high. Especially on set. You must've experienced that."

He coughs out a laugh. "Oh, yeah. I've been on the receiving end of a few rants. Usually for doing something like breathing."

"Then you know it's rarely to do with you."

"I know. Everyone's under pressure. I'd rather make people laugh, usually at me, as tension relief. Then they yell less."

"Well, don't try that with me."

"You don't like to laugh?"

"No time for that."

"Okay. Well, again, I apologize."

"Don't worry about it. Listen, it's after five. I've still got a few things to do but you can go."

"Are you sure? You don't need me to file anything or…"

"Nope. I'm good. See you tomorrow."

"See you tomorrow, then." He shifts in the doorway but hesitates before actually leaving. "Can I ask you something?"

I pull the pile of checks I need to sign across my desk. "Shoot."

"What do you like about this work?"

A laugh heavily laced with sarcasm is my immediate answer. "Ha. Nothing."

"Really? Then why do you do it?"

"I was kidding. Sort of. This work can be frustrating as hell, the days are endless, and I spend more time chasing my tail than getting anything done." I take a moment to let my gaze rove over the framed movie posters decorating the walls of my office, and pride replaces the irritation in my tone, because I was a key part of bringing every one of those projects to fruition. "But I can't imagine doing anything else."

"Why?"

"There's always a problem to solve, a challenge to face."

"Sounds like hell."

"I guess it would be for some people."

"Like, your work is never done."

"Never *boring*. And it is done when the movie wraps. Then I take a well-earned luxury vacation before moving on to the next one."

I sit back in my chair and really consider his question. "Actually, I do have a favorite part of the process. Preproduction, when I get to put the crew together. There's problem-solving and shit like budget concerns, but I love assembling the company, picturing how this particular group will mesh. How they'll challenge each other."

"You never wanted to be like, I don't know… the director?"

My head shake is definitive. "I'm not creative that way. A director has to have a vision. I couldn't do that. Don't have the confidence."

"Pfft. You're like the most confident person I've ever seen."

I point at him. "Because I'm clear about what I'm good at and what I'm not good at. I would not be good at reading a script and saying I'm going to put my stamp on this. Once someone has the ideas, I am the very good at making it happen. On time and on budget."

"Is it worth it?"

"Of course, it's worth it. We're fucking making movies." I pick up my pen. "Now get outta here before I think of something else for you to do."

# CHAPTER 9

> What is most important is to find peace and to share it with others. To have peace, you can begin by walking peacefully. Everything depends on your steps."""
>
> —Thich Nhat Hanh, *The Art of Mindful Living*

## SULLY

I'M FEELING SO MUCH BETTER after a week of work and an additional physical therapy workout that I want to do something for my friends to thank them for getting me off the couch and out the door.

Thinking that I'll make dinner—not easy with the broken leg, but I'm gradually figuring it out—I make some calls. Ford gets back to me first, letting me know that he's available, but Violet and Nate already have tickets to a play, and when Dani gets up, she tells me she's bartending at the Rumrunner tonight.

I almost call Ford back and tell him I want to postpone, but then I remember Violet's challenge. It really is time for the two of us to talk about what happened this summer and, hopefully, bury the hatchet. So I head to the store and buy a couple of fat steaks and a bunch of vegetables, planning to grill 'em all up.

After a nap on the couch with Skye, who promises not to tell Dani, I prep the food for cooking while I do my best to do the same for my opening speech.

*Ford, I truly didn't mean to get locked inside a Kmart overnight with Whit during Hurricane Beverly, but at the time it felt like I'd won the lottery.*

Nope, that gets into the Whitney thing too quickly.

*You know, Ford, I did a lot of thinking when I was on* Endless Summer—

Ugh. Don't want to think about the boat, either.

*Listen, man. You're my closest friend, but we've also been rivals in one way or another since the day we met. From who was faster on the playground to who got the girl—*

Guess it's going to be impossible to stay off of the Whitney topic.

Maybe I don't need to. He's dating again. Maybe that means he's over her.

Yeah, and if you believe that, Sully, you've only got one oar in the water.

Since this is getting me nowhere, I put on a mindfulness tape as I finish the dinner prep. When he shows up right on time with a six-pack in hand, my welcoming smile is relaxed.

"'Sup, man?" he asks.

"Just celebrating my first week of work with a steak dinner."

"Steak? You must be making the big bucks."

"Not exactly. If everyone had said yes, it'd be hamburgers, but since it's just you and me, I can afford steak."

"Their loss," he says.

"I do need your help to get this stuff outside, though."

"Oh, I get it. You just needed a sous chef."

"Pfft. You can't make anything that doesn't involve a microwave oven. But I do need your two hands."

As we move to the back porch and I get the fire going on the grill, we start with polite chat, asking about each other's families and such.

"Speaking of brothers," Ford says. "Working on *Lawson's Reach* has been surreal."

Dani had told me Ford was doing some work on the show, but I didn't think it was full-time. "Did you end up taking over for the boom guy, then?"

"Yeah." He shakes his head. "Dude was allergic to everything here and kept messing up takes with his sneezing, so he quit and went back to LA. I'd been doing second unit stuff, so the mixer was happy to bring me on."

"That's good, right?"

"Yeah. I mean, I was mixing on the second unit, but those days were few and far between. I think I need a few more credits before I can get a real mixing job." He finishes his beer and asks if I want another one.

"Sounds good. Take the steaks in while you're at it and stick 'em in the microwave."

"You want me to cook them in there?"

"God no, that's to hide them from the dog while they rest. Do *not* turn it on."

When he returns, the vegetables are ready, so we—or rather he—carries everything to the dining room.

After taking his first bite, Ford raises his glass to me. "To the chef. Always better than Longhorn Steakhouse."

My own mouth full, I roll my eyes at his version of a compliment.

"What were you saying about your brother and the show?"

"Yeah, so, it's weird. You know that Sheldon has been using stories my brother told him about us growing up as inspiration, right?"

Sheldon Williams—the creator of *Lawson's Reach*—grew up in Wallington and maintained his friendship with Ford's older brother, even after moving to Los Angeles. "Yeah. But I thought he changed things a lot."

"He does, mostly, but the two main guy characters—when I hear them talk and see the conflicts between them, I'm reminded of you and me. A lot."

I take a moment to fully chew the asparagus in my mouth before asking, "Like how?"

"Well, don't take this the wrong way, but the kid Lawson is kind of the Golden Boy, and his friend Parker is kind of a fuckup."

I put down my knife and fork and sit back in my chair. "Meaning, you're Lawson and I'm Parker?"

"Well, yeah. But it's more that everyone else sees them that way." He scrapes at the label on the beer bottle with his thumbnail as he continues. "Underneath all that, Lawson's full of self-doubt, and Parker's the one with his head on straight."

This was so not what I was expecting to hear that I'm struck dumb.

"And when they fight," he adds, "it *seems* like it's about a girl, but really it's about stuff that's unresolved between them."

"Like what kind of stuff?"

Ford shrugs, his eyes still on the beer bottle. "Like how Lawson couldn't take the risks he has without his friend's support, but it's hard for him to talk about, so his friend doesn't know that."

I have to clear my throat before I can ask, "By any chance, does this Parker kid think he'll never be as accomplished as his friend, so he quits trying?"

Ford finally meets my gaze. "Something like that."

We just sit in silence for a few moments until I say, "That must be weird. To have to stand there and listen to that."

He grunts. "Over and over again."

"What?" I gasp theatrically, hoping to shift the mood with a little humor. "They don't get it perfect on the first take?"

"Ugh, don't even talk to me about the number of takes. I may connect with the Lawson character, but the actor is so fucking vain. He seriously has to check the monitor to make sure his hair is well lit before we can move to a new setup."

No way am I going to say it aloud, but having roomed with both, I'd guess Ford spends more money on hair products each month than Dani has her entire life. Instead, I just smile and say, "How 'bout brownie sundaes for dessert?"

"I'll have to work out extra hard tomorrow, but hell yeah. It's worth it."

Unbelievably, it's October already, which to me is the best time for surfing. The tourists are gone, but the water is still warm enough that you don't need a wetsuit.

Going into the water is still off the table for me, but on Friday the doctor said my surgical wounds are healed enough that I can go to the beach. It'll be a pain to get the sand out of my removable cast, but I don't care. I miss seeing the ocean almost as much as I miss Mr. Jones and *Endless Summer*.

I also need a distraction from inappropriate thoughts about my boss.

Because my friends are awesome, they not only help me get there, they bring along a picnic. We caravan to Freeman Park, where you can drive on the beach, and set up for a lazy afternoon of watching the dog play in the waves, eating, and catching up.

Even though one of us is missing, it does my heart good to spend time with my best buddies. I don't want to be the one to bring her up, but when Violet gasps at something she reads in the Sunday paper, I have a feeling it's about Whitney.

"Everything okay?" Nate asks.

"I'm fine." Violet shakes her head slowly as she continues to read. "I just can't believe what I'm seeing."

Dani holds out her hand. "Lemme see."

"What is it?" Ford asks.

"Whitney's in the fucking society page." Violet shudders as she hands the paper over. "She always used to make fun of these pictures."

Dani frowns as she studies the paper. "Yikes. It's like someone hit her over the head with a Cinderella stick."

Ford peers over her shoulder. "She's gone to the dark side."

Violet falls back onto the beach blanket and covers her face with her arms. "Before you know it, she'll have a house on the Azalea Festival tour and think the Garden Party is the social event of the year. And she'll claim that being an Azalea Belle was her favorite thing ever."

"When she told us she hated every minute of it," Ford adds. "Complained that getting all dolled up and wandering around some estate dressed in a hoop skirt was sexist, racist, *and* classist."

"Which I could've told her," Dani says, tossing the newspaper on the sand.

"I thought her mom made her do it," Violet says.

Something occurs to me. "Does anyone know if she's going back to work?"

"Probably going to start selling real estate with her parents instead of doing hair and makeup," Ford says.

"Can I see it?" I ask.

Dani hands me the paper. "I hate to say it, but maybe these are her true colors."

As I take in Whitney's pixelated image, I can't bring myself to say what I'm thinking. *Maybe we drove her to this.*

Violet opens the cooler and studies its contents. "It can't last. She'll leave him."

"Should y'all try and let her know that we'll be here to pick up the pieces?" Ford asks.

"What's this 'y'all'?" Dani asks. "What about you?"

Ford frowns. "She doesn't answer my calls."

"She rarely answers when I call, and she always has an excuse for why she can't hang out. Not that I want to spend time with Hardy," Dani mutters.

A quick glance at the photo of Whitney posing with her new husband at some fundraising gala or other is more than I need to see. After I close the paper, though, something on the back page catches my eye. "Huh. There's a notice"—I pause to finish reading—"Man. Her parents are petitioning the planning board about a new development over by the battleship."

"Isn't that, like, a swamp over there?" Ford asks.

Before anyone can answer, Nate waves at someone walking toward us on the sand.

I shield my eyes against the sun, now low on the horizon. "Who's that?"

"Hey, George! Hey, Tina!" Violet calls.

"Aren't those the people that rode up to Raleigh with us after Hurricane Beverly?" I whisper to Ford.

"Yeah," Ford says, his jaw tightening.

"Sully and Ford, you remember George Bronson and Tina Fiorentino?" Dani prompts.

"Right," I say with a wave. "The writers from *Lawson's Reach*."

Everyone else but me stands to greet them.

"Y'all are back already?" Ford asks.

"They're shooting the first episode we wrote, and we get to watch!" Tina sits in a folding chair. "We're working on one about a hurricane now."

George sits next to her. "We were going to put something in about characters getting stuck overnight in a Kmart."

"But we're going to save that for its own episode. It's just so romantic."

George clears his throat. "Um, as long as it's okay with you guys."

Ford catches my eye with a *What'd I tell you?* look, which weirdly makes me feel better about the whole thing, because at least we're on the same page. "Sure, whatever you gotta do."

It's in that moment that George seems to notice the brace on my leg. "What happened to you, man?"

"My sailboat got rammed by a motorboat and I broke my tibia."

"Oh, no, that's horrible." Tina's hand goes to her chest.

"Yeah, it pretty much sucked. But I'm on the mend. Coulda been worse."

Violet breaks out the picnic basket and as people start to eat, conversation splinters. Tina catches Violet up on what's happening at the inn her grandparents used to own, while Ford and Dani talk about *Lawson's Reach* with George.

Nate settles down next to me and hands me a plate full of food.

"I could've gotten it myself," I protest.

"Don't blame me," he says. "Violet did it."

"Well, thanks," I say before digging in.

"Any news on how long before you can surf again?" he asks between mouthfuls.

"Doc said its healing like it's supposed to, and as long as I keep up with the PT, I'll be back out there next summer."

"Next summer!" Nate says. "Jeez. That's almost a year."

"I'm hoping he assumes that nobody surfs in the winter."

"Me too. But hey, I've been meaning to tell you. I put my boards in your shed when I moved back from California. If you're not going to be using yours until next spring, you need to let me pay for the storage."

"You don't have to do that. I'll be needing them soon enough."

"I hope that's the case. But in the meantime, I'm either

giving you your key back and getting my own shed or paying the rent."

"Do they all fit in there?"

"Yeah, long as I keep it organized."

Thinking about how Vi compared filing documents to sorting surfboards makes me smile, even as the stack of bills I need to pay looms large in my mind. "All right. I can use the extra cash. But Ronnie says March is a possibility. Her workouts are tough, but she promises it'll pay off."

"You need help?"

"Naw. I'm so sick of needing help from people. It's just hard to motivate myself after a long day at work. Even though I just sit on my ass all day. And my days are about to get even longer because we start shooting this week."

"Yeah, I know. We're working on your movie. Well, Vi is." He looks over at her and gets all goofy-eyed. "She just tells me what to do."

"Hey, she's older than you, isn't she?"

"Vi? Uh, yeah. By a few years. Why?"

"Just wondering."

Aaand my thoughts are back to Helen. It's hard to say how old she is—not that I'd ever ask—but I suspect the age gap between us is bigger than the one between Nate and Vi. Anyway, he may claim she tells him what to do, but they're partners.

Helen is my boss.

Something I need to keep reminding myself of.

# CHAPTER 10

"Let me give you a piece of advice here. You want to make it in this business, you don't have time for a personal life, much less a relationship."

—*Swimming With Sharks*

## HELEN

THE LAST WEEK of pre-production is always a scramble. Costume fittings inevitably reveal that actors lied about their measurements, which leads to requests for money to replace wasted fabric. Then there's always some housing issue. This week it was fleas in one of the rentals, which meant we had to find an alternative as well as get the deposit back from the landlord of the infested property. The toughest challenge, though, was replacing the computer consultant. The original guy totally flaked and double-booked himself—or got a better offer, more likely. Sully earned his salary for the week when he used his parents' connections at the university to find us a local professor to step in. Saving us from flying someone in and putting them up.

And speaking of Sully, I'm quite proud of the fact that I

have not only stopped objectifying him—at least in my waking hours; not even I can control my dreams—but I have not yelled at him once this week. Okay, maybe once. But he yelled right back, so we're even.

My final meeting of the day—and the week—is with Glenda, the movie's production office coordinator. Between the two of us, we make sure that the plans made in pre-production come to fruition. For instance, I hire the crew; she makes sure the crew gets where we need them to be. When the director wants a change, I wrangle the budget, robbing Peter to pay Paul, while she disseminates the new schedule.

Technically, I'm her supervisor, but because we've worked together multiple times and our jobs overlap so much, I see what we do as more collaborative.

No matter who's the boss, if the UPM and the PC don't jibe, production grinds to a halt. Glenda and I may seem like chalk and cheese, but we use that to our advantage. She's refined, grew up upper middle class in Connecticut. I'm scrappy, grew up poor in Queens. People call her Glenda the Good Witch, and since I'm the bad cop, I'm pretty sure they call me Helen the Scary as Hell Witch. Or worse.

But hey, I don't need people to like me.

Everyone except for the tight circle of female department heads I've managed to assemble for this show, that is. I like them and want them to know I've got their backs, so the final task of the day is choosing the location for tonight's meetup. It'll likely be the last Friday we actually leave the office before midnight, so we need to take advantage of that.

"Dive or upscale?" Glenda asks. "Drag show or Heavy Metal Bingo? Beer or cocktail?"

"How do you know so much about the bars in town? We've only been here for a few weeks."

She shrugs. "I make a point to take a few locals out for a drink and get the lowdown. Then I can make recommendations."

"While Heavy Metal Bingo intrigues, somewhere quiet might be better. And downtown, so it's close to housing." Most of the actors are in beach houses, while the crew is split between the one corporate suite hotel in the county and various furnished apartments that locals rent out.

"Let's do 125 Market Street, then. It's supposed to have comfy seating."

I jot the name into my Filofax. "If that's also the address, it should be easy for everyone to find."

"Meet there at what... seven? I'll spread the word on my way back to my office." She stands and pats the heavy three-ring binder she carries everywhere. "I've got to stash the bible, and then I'm out of here."

I scan my own office. Sully left early today to go to PT, so the usual piles of things I could be attending to are higher than usual. Interesting how useful he's made himself in just a couple weeks.

"Earth to Helen." Glenda's voice breaks into my reverie.

"Sorry." I gesture at my desk. "Obviously, I could stay here all night, but I need a break."

"See you downtown, then."

## SULLY

Even though I totally forgot to ask Helen if it was okay for me to take time off for my PT appointment today, she didn't give me a hard time about it. In fact, she said that I might as well take the rest of the day off since it was the last chance we'd have at a Friday evening for a while. Apparently, this show has a lot of night shoots.

Normally, I hate working nights because it makes it so hard to get in time on my board before the beach gets crowded. Of course, that's not happening anytime soon. A noon-to-midnight schedule will have its challenges, but it'll make getting to doctor's appointments easier.

When I finish up at Veronica's, I find myself at a bit of a loss. I can't take my boat out or swim or surf. My friends will all be working for at least a few more hours, so I guess I could make dinner for everyone.

Then I have a better idea.

Even though Helen's worked in Wallington once before, she probably doesn't know the town well. I could take her out for a drink. Show her around.

Not like a date.

But maybe like a date.

I mean, some businesses frown on fraternizing among employees, but people on movie crews sleep together all the time. Especially when they're working out of town. It's like a free-for-all of sex.

And even though Helen hasn't said anything, I think she might be attracted to me. I've caught her checking me out more than once. At least I think I have.

Can't hurt to ask. Worst she can say is no, right?

## HELEN

Naturally, I get caught by a series of phone calls before I make it out the door to meet the ladies, but I do manage to put out the fires post haste and turn the answering machine on by five o'clock.

Just as I'm closing my door, Sully walks into the outer office. "What are you doing here?"

He flashes me a discombobulating grin. "I work here."

"Not right now you don't," I say as I turn the key in the lock. "We're closed for the weekend. It won't happen again for the next five weeks, so don't get used to it."

Instead of turning to leave, he takes a step closer to me. "Did you—do you need something from my office?"

"Oh, no."

"Well, see you Monday. Six thirty sharp." He doesn't move, so I add, "That's a.m., not p.m."

"Right." He looks nervous all of a sudden, which makes me nervous.

"Well, I'm going to—"

"Do you want to go get a drink?" he asks at the same time.

When he doesn't say anything further, I blurt, "What—like a date?"

His cheeks pink up, and he squeezes the handles of his crutches. "Yeah. If you want."

"Oh," I say, shaking my head so rapidly my brain sloshes around inside my skull. "No. That's not—"

"Oh—okay." Sully takes a half step back, his head bobbing in time with mine. "You don't have to—I mean, it's fine. I just thought—you're an attractive woman, and I'd love to take you out. But if that makes you uncomfortable, then—"

"It's not that. It's… I'm married." The words pop out of my mouth so fast I don't even see them coming.

"Y-You are?"

"Yep," I say, even as I curse myself. Lying to him can only end badly. But it was that or say yes to a drink with Sully, and we all know how that would end. "All… married up."

"Oh, well. I'm sorry. I mean. I'm sorry I assumed that—anyway. Good for you. And for him."

*Goddammit.* He's even cuter when he's flustered.

"Okay, well. I'll, uh, see you Monday."

"Yep."

"Unless you need me to do anyth—"

"No, no. You need to rest up this weekend." My voice rises in pitch and volume as the words tumble out of my mouth. "Next week'll be tough. We get here before the crew starts and leave after they're done."

"You said that. I got it," he says, a wrinkle forming between his brows.

"Okay," I say as I actually clap my hands, like I'm some sort of married cheerleader now. "Well. Have a good weekend."

"You too," he says as he, blessedly, backs out the door.

I shut the door behind him and lean against it, whispering, "What the fuck was that, O'Neill?"

Twenty minutes later I plop down next to Glenda in a cozy seating nook in the trendy-ish bar and say hello to the other women already well into a first round. When a cocktail waitress appears, I say, "A whiskey sour and another round for these ladies."

"Thanks, Helen," costume coordinator Sherry Yorn says, raising a half-full glass of some sort of white wine.

"Same," says Kara Friedman, our set decorator.

Glenda raises a martini glass half-filled with a bright green liquid. "To another show."

"Where are Gemma and Nora?" I ask.

"They're coming," Sherry says of the makeup and hair department heads. "They had a last-minute consult with the sound department about wigs and hats."

"Good times," says Kara, draining her glass.

"Can't have all the good times until we're all represented," Glenda says with a pout.

After accepting my drink and thanking the waitress, I raise the glass. "Agreed. Got to get together before we can stick together."

"And that'll be more important than ever on this show," Kara says.

"Why so?" I sit back in my chair to take a restorative sip of my drink, not sure if I want to hear the answer or not.

"This show is all computers and car chases. I hate that shit. It makes the men even more obnoxious than usual."

"Seriously," says Sherry. "I had to listen to the second AD talk about engines over lunch today. I thought I was going to fall asleep in my salad."

"And the way they talk about computers. Like I couldn't possibly know what a motherboard is," adds Kara.

Glenda shakes her head. "Or the difference between a hard disk and a floppy disk."

"Um"—Sherry taps her nose—"what *is* the difference between a hard disk and a floppy disk? I mean, in my experience, hard is always better than floppy!"

We all cheer to that, and I relax farther into my seat.

Until Sully walks in the door.

"Shit," I hiss, doing my best to hide behind Sherry.

"Hey, isn't that your office PA?"

I grab her arm and lower it. "Don't wave at him, he'll—"

"Hey, y'all," Sully says to the group, all friendly and easygoing until he sees me. "Oh, hi, Hel—uh, O'Nei—I mean, boss."

"Do you want to join us?" Sherry asks, looking him up and down appreciatively.

"Oh, no, no. I'll leave you to it. I'm meeting some friends."

He maneuvers to the bar, the crowd edging out of the way of his crutches.

Glenda whaps me on the arm. "Why was he all weird with you?"

I slap both palms over my face. "I might've told him I was married."

"What? Why?" Kara asks.

Glenda narrows her eyes at me. "Because she likes him."

"Because he asked me out," I hiss. "And I panicked."

Sherry's expression is dialed to skeptical. "What's wrong with him? He looks pretty fly to me."

"What's wrong is that I'm his boss."

"Never stopped any of my bosses from hitting on me," mutters Kara.

"Oooh, are we telling creepy boss stories?" Gemma says as she squeezes into a spot on the couch next to Sherry. "Shove over, girl."

"I've got a couple of those." Nora perches on the arm of Kara's chair. "What are we drinking?"

"Whatever the hell you want. I'm buying the next round." Glenda waves at the waitress. "I highly recommend the Appletini."

The waitress takes orders, and we spend a few minutes looking for a chair for Nora. I use the opportunity to change the subject. "I've been meaning to ask, Nora—how come you didn't go back for the next season of *The Practice*? Not that I'm complaining. I'm happy to have you."

Glenda swats at me. "Helen! What if they didn't ask her back?"

"She told me she left, but I never heard why. Just curious," I add.

Nora shrugs. "I just couldn't handle the TV schedule."

"Seems like it'd be nice to have a regular gig, though," Sherry says. "And in town. I mean, you could actually, like, live in your own apartment."

"Yeah, that's why I took it." Nora sighs. "But I hated it. It just got relentless. Months and months of the same fucking people, the same fucking commute. Even at home—I got so sick of the same gym and restaurants and neighbors."

"Huh." Sherry, the youngest woman in the group, rests her chin on her palm. "I never thought of it like that."

"I get it," I say. "I can't imagine working at the pace I do for eight or nine months straight. I'd rather go at it a thousand percent and then get a few weeks or months to shut down."

"Too much of a commitment?" asks Glenda. "Like movies are an affair and TV is a relationship?"

I shoot a knowing smirk at Glenda, who's been married for at least ten years. "Like movies are an adventure and TV's a job."

When the waitress arrives with the next round of drinks, Nora grabs hers and raises her glass. "To adventure?"

"To adventure!" we chorus in return.

As I'm clinking glasses, I catch Sully raising a beer glass to me from across the bar. I give him a nod, drain my glass, and signal the waitress for another round.

*To adventure, indeed.*

## SULLY

Even though it's good to be out with my friends, my attention doesn't stray far from the group of women from our show. They're all attractive, but my eyes just keep tracking back to Helen. She's just so impressive. Like Violet and Dani combined, turned up to eleven.

It's probably best that she's married. She's too good for me. Too smart, too accomplished, too driven. Too fucking gorgeous.

Funny thing is, she's the polar opposite of Whitney. Where Whit is soft, Helen's tough. Where Whit is self-effacing, Helen's in your face. The only thing they have in common is blond hair, but Whitney's is natural, and Helen's comes from a bottle.

Not that it makes her any less sexy.

Which cannot be said, unfortunately, for the girl Ford brought along tonight, whose voice is driving me up the fucking wall. I don't know how Ford can stand it. I mean, this girl—Bitsy, I think is her name—is cute, but when she opens her mouth, it's like a dentist's drill into your skull.

And it's not just that she has a New York accent. Helen has

one that doesn't drive me crazy. At least not in a bad way. Her low tones are sexy as hell. Bitsy, on the other hand, sounds like that character on *The Nanny*. She seems nice, and I'm glad Ford's getting out there, but I sure as hell hope it doesn't last between them.

Speaking of getting out there, I've been enjoying watching Helen have an extra-good time tonight, laughing with friends.

Unfortunately, when she gets up from her seat, she sways like she may have had a little too much to drink. When she weaves toward the restrooms and a guy follows her, I'm on my feet. Or foot.

I may not be a hundred percent, but I'm not letting some asshole assault my drunk boss.

Just as I'd feared, by the time I get there, the guy's got her up against the wall. He's not touching her yet, but he's leaning way too close.

"Hey, buddy," I call out. "Back off."

He turns to face me, a sneer on his face. "Mind your own business, dude."

"She is my business."

He turns back to Helen, who seems to be patting him on the chest. "What do you say, hot stuff? Want to get out of here?"

"She's married. Tell him, Helen."

She giggles and cups her hands around her mouth as if to share a secret. "I'm actually not. I just told him I was."

Unfortunately, I can hear her loud and clear.

The guy takes her by the upper arm and begins to steer her toward the back exit. "She's obviously just not into *you*, asshole."

"O'Neill!"

She turns to face me, but the guy's still dragging her down the hall. I'm on their heels, trying to figure out if I can take the guy when she wriggles out of his hold.

"I'm not going home with you," she says, her voice slurred.

"Come on, baby," he says. "It'll be fun."

She turns to look at him, seeming to consider it.

"O'Neill," I say softly. "Do you really want to go home with this guy?"

She sighs—a pitiful sound—and turns back to me.

"No. I want to go home with you." She sticks out her lower lip in a pout. "But I can't."

The guy looks like he's going to make another go at her, so I limp closer. "Mister, you have one chance to walk out that door. Alone."

When he doesn't move, I balance on one crutch and lift the other. "I have no problem using this as a weapon."

"Whatever. Old bag's not worth it, anyway."

I'd like to pop him one in his nasty mouth, but as he passes me to go back into the bar, he shoulders me out of the way, knocking me off balance and making me drop a crutch.

One hand on the wall, I try to bend down to retrieve it, but Helen gets to it before I do. As she hands it to me, she sways a bit. After I shove it under my armpit, a hand lands on my chest.

Doing my best to ignore it, I say, "Let's get you home, okay?"

Instead of answering, her palm widens over my left pec, and she nestles in close to whisper, "I'm sorry I lied."

"You didn't have to," I say softly. "You could've just told me you weren't into me."

"But *that* would be lying," she whispers.

Her gaze roams from my eyes to my mouth, like she's thinking about kissing me. I'm totally tempted, but the whiskey on her breath reminds me that the woman isn't all here. No way am I going to take advantage of that after I just chased off another dude for trying to do the same thing.

So I do the right thing.

"Come on, O'Neill. Let's go find your friends."

# CHAPTER 11

"Is it being prepared to do the right thing, whatever the cost? Isn't that what makes a man?"

"Hmmm... Sure, that and a pair of testicles."

–*The Big Lebowski*

## HELEN

TIME TO PAY THE PIPER.

I spend Saturday nursing a hangover—aka eating junk food and flipping back and forth between HBO and the Million Dollar Movie—and Sunday catching up on paperwork I should've done Saturday.

Both days I'm deep in denial of what happened in that bar hallway. Because obviously that almost-kiss was just a result of alcohol plus pheromones plus sex drought. Plus, there's no way that adorable guy would be into a mildly-attractive-on-a-good-day woman ten years his senior.

But now I have to face the man that not only saved me from having to fight off that jerk's advances myself—or worse, being the victim of an assault—but who behaved like a perfect gentleman when I threw myself at him. Thank goodness he's a good guy, or this morning would be even more awkward.

I'm not sure if it's a good thing or a bad thing that I have to see him even earlier than usual, since it's the first day of shooting, and I always like to be the first one on set. I'm a rip-the-Band-Aid-off kind of gal, so I gird myself for the encounter the way I prepare to do anything difficult: head-banging music on the drive to work.

"Rearviewmirror" on repeat revs me up like nothing else, so I rock out through the security gate, whip into my parking space like a boss, screech to a stop, and am rarin' to go as I hop out of the car.

And run straight into the solid chest I've dreamed about all weekend.

"Jesus, O'Neill!" Sully yelps as I stumble backward. "You almost took me out."

"You shouldn't sneak up on people like that," I growl. "You scared the shit out of me."

"I can't sneak up on anybody on these things." His grin is wicked as he raises a crutch. "But your ears must still be ringing. You could hear your radio from a mile away. I can't believe you listen to Pearl Jam."

"What, do you think I'm too old to like them?" Pissed that I've already lost whatever nerve I built up on the drive in, I head for the office, hoping he'll ignore my question. "Walk with me. We don't have time to stand around gabbing about musical preferences."

The length of his stride means that even on crutches he can easily keep up with me unless I'm running, so I launch into instructions for the day as we navigate the front doors and stop by the copy room to grab the faxes. "Chances are there'll be script changes from Friday's table read, so that's a priority. You triage the rest of these messages and cover the phones while I go over to set. Keep your walkie close in case I need anything."

Once inside the empty office—the rest of the staff won't be in for hours—I make myself stop and face the man who hasn't said a word beyond a handful of "Yups" and "Got its."

"So, uh, before I head over there, I just wanted to apologize about Friday."

He tips his head to the side. "Apologize?"

My hand flies up in the space between us, like it could erase the memories of his sex-on-the-beach scent that somebody ought to bottle. Or the rock-hard expanse of his chest under my palm. "Whatever I did or said, it was fueled entirely by alcohol, so I'd appreciate it if we could just forget it ever happened."

Full lips flatten into a line. I can't deal with an argument, so I barrel on. "Glenda told me that you scared off some asshole who was hitting on me, so thanks for that as well. For the record, I do not typically get drunk when I'm working. It was just..." *Me trying to squelch all the troublesome feelings I have for you* would be the truth, but I go with "Drinks I didn't realize were so strong on an empty stomach. It won't happen again."

He looks like he wants to say something, and a bunch of emotions flicker across his face—could be disgust, could be disappointment, who knows. Then he just wipes a hand down his face, smoothing it all away. "Yep. Got it."

"Got it? We're good, then?"

"Yup. We're good."

"Good. So, big day. Let's get to it." I grab my walkie-talkie from the charger, drop my purse in a desk drawer, and grab a legal pad. "I'll stay at the stage for the first few setups. Buzz me if you need me."

He takes in a breath like he's going to make a speech or something, but then he blows it out. "I'll do that."

Later in the week, a day with a crazy schedule involving three company moves is made crazier by the fact that my early shift accountant is three hours late.

I've been through emails and phone messages from the night before and put out the necessary fires. Now, I need to get to the set. Sully may be distracting as hell, but today I'm thankful I've got a reliable office PA.

"I called John and let him know he might have an extra hour or so of work today if Dee doesn't show," I yell to Sully as I pack up my messenger bag. "If you have time to start entering yesterday's line items, that'll help."

Sully rolls by my office doorway, a banker's box full of folders in his lap. "Will do."

"I just can't believe Dee wouldn't even call. That's not like—" Before I can finish my sentence, the phone rings.

"You need me to get that?" Sully calls.

"No, I have a minute." After pressing the flashing button, I tuck the receiver between my ear and shoulder. "Production. O'Neill."

"Helen, it's Dee. I'm so sorry I'm not there."

Her usually chipper tone has been muted. In fact, she sounds congested, like she's been crying, so I ask, "Is everything okay?"

"It will be. I hope. Van was throwing up all night, and then his fever spiked to over a hundred and four." She sniffs. "The pediatrician on call told me to take him to the emergency room. They got some fluids in him, and his temperature came down, but we just got home."

"That sounds terrible."

"My husband's out of town, but I can see if I can get a neighbor to come over and—"

"No, no, Dee. You stay home with your baby. We can manage here."

"Are you sure?"

"Of course. Maybe keep your phone handy in case John or

Sully have any questions, though. You just get some rest and take care of your son. And keep me posted, okay?"

"I will. Thank you so much, Helen."

"Don't worry about it. I'll see you when he's better."

After I hang up, I grab my bag and car keys.

"Everything okay?" Sully asks.

I fill him in and ask him to warn John that he might have a few days with overtime on the books. "We'll have to make some adjustments to the budget too."

"Because of the overtime? Can't that just come out of what we would've paid Dee?"

"She'll get paid anyway. They need the money. It's not like we get sick days." I shake my head as I head for the door. "I could never have kids."

"Because you don't like them?"

I pause, a hand on the doorknob. "What do you think would happen if I had to leave early?"

"Uh… nothing?"

"Exactly." I open the door. "See you later."

"Not if I see you first," Sully calls.

I shoot him the bird, but I'm laughing.

# CHAPTER 12

"Understanding the other is understanding yourself, and understanding yourself is understanding the other person. Everything must begin with you."

–Thich Nhat Hanh

## SULLY

FOUR DAYS into principal photography working for Helen, and I vow I'll never complain about the sound department again. Fourteen-hour days are hard, especially when you have to be out in nasty weather, but if I could walk, I'd trade them in a minute for sixteen-hour days moving paper and numbers around.

It's hard to complain when Helen drives herself harder than everyone around her, but the schedule the woman keeps is brutal. Even for someone who isn't nursing an injury while keeping a lid on his attraction to a woman who's off-limits.

Things are super busy the first few days of shooting, meaning that Helen and I are like ships passing in the night. Not sure if it's on purpose, but every time I find her in the office, she leaves. Or gives me an errand to run. I don't think she's mad about what happened Friday, but I don't believe that she's not attracted to me either. I'm just not sure why it's such a big deal.

When she finally says we can close the office today, I should go home and do PT exercises, but all I want to do is drink beer and watch whatever stupid crap is on TV. Something I never used to do.

My life before the accident revolved around my boat, the beach, my friends, food, and work. In that order. Missing half of those things, I can't seem to motivate beyond getting myself to work every day. I don't think I'm as depressed as I was a few weeks ago, but I'm still not quite myself.

When I pull into the driveway of Dani's house, I'm surprised to find Nate and Ford in her garage moving stuff around. It's still a process to get in and out of the car, so by the time I hobble over, they've cleared a space and are setting up equipment.

"What are y'all doing?" I ask, even though it's obvious that they're planning to work out.

As he unfolds a thick mat like we used in high school gym class, Nate says, "We were complaining to Dani about how much a gym membership costs, and Ford's cousin was giving this stuff away, so she said we could move it in here since neither of us has room in our apartments."

My eyes narrow in suspicion. "This doesn't have anything to do with me and my PT?"

Ford returns from his car, barbells in hand. "I mean, if you want to bring your pansy ass and your little rubber bands out here and try to keep up, you're welcome to."

Nate winces theatrically. "I don't know if it's a good idea. We wouldn't want you to strain yourself or anything."

"You assholes couldn't act your way out of a paper bag. This is about me not doing my exercises."

Nate drags a weight bench across the floor. "I wouldn't know anything about that."

"I just need somewhere to work out." Ford sets an ancient-looking boombox on a folding table and looks around for a place to plug it in. "And if you're not using that mix CD I went to the trouble of making, I'll take it back."

Ten minutes later, music is blaring, and the three of us are rotating through the stations they've set up. I can't jump rope, obviously, but I can do a full upper-body workout. I've been pretty good about doing ankle stretches during the workday, but on the mat I can work my hip flexors and quads too.

I'll never admit it to these assholes, but between the music and the banter and the company, it is a lot easier to get through the rest of the routine.

That doesn't mean I enjoy all the exercises I'm supposed to do. I mean, I don't think I could pick up a marble with my toes and put it in a cup *before* I broke my leg. My stupid foot is shaking with effort when Ford asks me something.

"Sorry, what?" Losing my focus, I accidentally kick over the cup. "God*dam*mit!"

"Man, you really have lost your marbles." Ford laughs as he squats effortlessly to help me clean up the mess. "I said, how is it working with the Gorgon?"

"The Gorgon? What's that?"

Nate grabs a marble from under a bench and drops it into the cup. "That's what people call Helen."

"That's kind of mean." After carefully setting the cup aside, I grab a resistance band and loop it around the ball of my foot.

"Well? Is she or isn't she?" Ford prods.

His question awakens the memory of her petite and surprisingly warm hand on my chest. A twinge from my knee —which I probably just overstretched—brings me back to the present. I'm not going to admit it to these guys, but I'm a little obsessed with my boss. She's the smartest woman I've ever spent any time around. Like if she were president, she'd have all the world's problems solved in a week.

Is it weird that I find that sexy as hell?

"Earth to Sullivan," Ford says, flicking a finger on my forehead.

"Ow," I say, slapping his hand away. "Leave me alone. I'm injured."

"That's why I didn't knock you off the bench, you doof." He takes a step back and cocks his head. "Whoa. You like her."

I huff out a sound that I hope sounds like denial. "What is this, eighth grade?"

Nate steps up next to Ford. "Yeah, I think he's right."

Sighing, I point a finger at Nate. "Do not say anything to your girlfriend."

Right on cue, Violet steps into the open garage doorway. "Don't say anything to his girlfriend about what?" When Nate jogs over and tries to put his arm around her, she dodges away. "Yuck. You're all sweaty."

He catches her hand and kisses it. "You didn't mind that this morning."

She blushes. "That was different."

"Sweat is sweat, baby," he says, enveloping her in a hug.

She groans even as her arms circle his neck and their lips meet.

"Gross!" Ford and I howl in unison.

After what seems like forever, Violet breaks the kiss. "What am I not supposed to know?"

Nate murmurs something in her ear.

"No way!" Violet gasps. "She's, like, ten years older than us."

"She is not," I say, even though I'm not sure exactly how old Helen is.

Ford points at my leg. "Can you even have sex with your leg like that?"

I lever myself up off the bench, grab a crutch, and drop my PT supplies in my gym bag. "She is my boss, y'all. We are not having sex. I may think she's hot, but I need this job."

"You think Helen's hot?" Dani asks from behind me.

"Ugh! I hate you people."

After I grab my bag and my other crutch, I grumble, "Outta my way, girl. I need a shower."

She moves, but as I hobble down the hall, she calls, "Okay, but if you want dinner, you'll have to spill."

Man, I need to get my own place to live.

I'm in the zone, riding the gnarliest wave ever when I hear my mom's voice.

"Hello, hello! Anybody home?"

It's so weird to see her surfing next to me that I step right off my board. Into thin air, falling in slo-mo, arms flailing, not toward the water or the ground, but toward the wooden interior of my boat. Instead of making impact, I fall through it. Into warm water. Little pink paw pads surrounded by black fur swim ahead of me. I'm desperate to get to them, but they're always out of reach. I swim and swim under water, but when I finally come up for air, he's gone.

And… I'm in my bed. When I turn my head, the hands on the clock pointing to the ten and the three have me panicking until I remember that it's Saturday. I'm still not sleeping great because it's hard to get comfortable with my brace. Between that and the long workdays, sleeping in on the weekend is the only way to catch up.

After I heave myself out of bed and into the hallway, I realize my mom's voice wasn't just in my dream. She's actually in the house, talking to Dani in the kitchen, but I can't quite make out what they're saying. This has me peeing, brushing my teeth, and getting dressed in record speed—for a guy on crutches, that is.

The two of them conspiring to fix me is all I need.

Unfortunately, by the time I make it to the kitchen, they've obviously been at it long enough to make trouble.

"He was really depressed, Mrs. Calloway."

"I know, but are you sure being back to work is a good idea? I'd hate to have him reinjure the leg."

"My doctor signed off on it, Mom. You can ask me, you know," I add, unable to keep the grump out of my voice.

Dani's cheeks are red as she backs toward her bedroom. "I've got to, uh, do some… things."

After her door closes, I jut my chin at the bags covering the counter. "What's all this?"

"I've been so busy with the start of the semester, I haven't been able to help much. But"—she begins pulling food out of the grocery bags—"I did do some research. All these are foods that help promote the healing of broken bones."

She lays out piles of fruit and vegetables, jars of vitamins, and some cans. "Leafy greens and brassicas for Vitamin K, fruit for Vitamin C. Then there's yogurt and cheese for calcium. Eggs for zinc. You also need to be eating lots of lean protein every single day. I'll bring some fresh fish by when I can, but I got you some smoked salmon and canned tuna. No Coca-Cola, though. Too much sugar is bad, and there's some other thing in soda that's bad for you."

"You didn't need to do all this, Mom."

She waves that down as she begins to put things away. "I know you don't have a membership to Costco, and vitamins are so much cheaper there. Do y'all have a blender?"

"I think so." I shuffle over to the cabinets and start opening and closing them.

She holds up a container of protein powder and a bag of mixed frozen fruit. "Easy-peasy to make a protein smoothie with these and some juice or milk. You've got to build muscle as well as help the bones heal."

Growing up, I always got the feeling that my parents wished I were different. More like my older brother, who excelled in everything with ease, or Ford, who worked hard to overcome every challenge. I mean, the guy actually took a class in audio engineering at Cal Tech. And understood it. Compared to the two of them, my parents always said I was "wasting my potential."

Ever since the accident, things have changed. My mom calls, like, every other day to ask how I'm feeling, and my dad has even checked in a few times—though he mostly bugs me about contacting a lawyer. I can't figure out if their newfound concern is a good thing or a bad thing.

"Last thing is Vitamin D." She faces me, hands on hips, her expression closer to what I'm used to. Slightly suspicious. "Are you getting outside?"

"Actually, we went to the beach last weekend."

"Are you allowed to do that?"

"Mom. I am an adult."

She looks like she's about to argue so I add, "Do you think I'd do something to jeopardize being able to surf again?"

"I'm sorry. You're right. It's just—" She breaks off with a sigh. "I worry about you."

"I've been taking care of myself just fine for the past seven years, you know."

She nods, but her chin wobbles.

Hobbling closer, I set my crutches against the counter, and perch on the edge of a barstool. Grabbing her hand, I squeeze until she looks at me. "I'm going to be okay."

Nodding faster, she presses her lips together. After a few breaths, she whispers, "I know. You just gave me a scare. And it made me realize what's really important."

"And what's that?"

"Life." She circles her hands in the air. "You've always been so good at... well, living. You were such an active little boy, always wanted to be outside running around, swimming, boating." Biting her lip, she picks up the canned fish and turns back to the cabinets. "Seeing you in that hospital bed, looking like you might not survive, scared me to death. I can't lose my baby. It's not right."

"Even if your baby is a lazy good-for-nothing?"

Her head snaps back to me, her chin high. "I never said that."

"You kind of did. Not those exact words, but—"

She crosses her arms over her chest. "It's a parent's job to push their kids."

"Even if it's in a direction that kid doesn't want to go?"

"I was just worried you wouldn't—"

"'Live up to my potential'? That is a direct quote."

"Yes, well—"

"And where is Dad?

She looks toward the door like he might materialize any moment. "He…"

"Has nothing to say to the college dropout?" I supply when she doesn't finish.

"He doesn't always know what to say to you, it's true, but—"

"How about"—I adopt a gruff voice to mimic his—"'I don't know why you can't be more like your brother.'"

"Sweetheart, we just worry about you." Her words may be sugary, but her tone sours them. "And I guess we don't understand what it is you want."

"Well, I'll tell you. How I treat people and the world around me is more important than 'making my mark.' I'm sorry if that's not enough for you."

Her jaw drops briefly, but then she clears her throat. "Do you really think that's how we feel?"

"Y'all make it pretty obvious. But I'll tell you what, I am self-sufficient"—I swipe a hand in the direction of my lame leg—"or I was until this happened. I don't ask you for anything."

I tip my chin at the now-empty bags lying all over the

counter. "And here you are second-guessing me again. Bringing me food like I can't take care of myself."

"I'm not—"

"Aren't you?"

"Dani said that you were depressed," she says, her voice uncharacteristically whiny.

"I was. I am still, probably, okay? I mean, I lost my damn boat. The boat I spent years refurbishing. I dragged my poor cat out on the water with me so I wouldn't be alone, and because of that, he drowned." I tick the rest off on my fingers. "I can't walk. I can't swim. I can't surf. So how 'bout giving me a fucking break?"

She just blinks at me, seemingly surprised as I am at my outburst.

After a few long breaths, I hold up a hand. "I'm sorry, I shouldn't take my frustration out on you."

"No. You're right. I need to give you more credit. You *have* taken care of yourself all these years. And you did an amazing job with *Endless Summer*." She grabs my hand. "And I'm so sorry you lost it, and especially Mr. Jones."

"But I'm very grateful that we didn't lose you. And all this —" She squeezes my hand before releasing it and turning her energy to folding up the paper bags. "This is just my way of telling you I care about you, and I want to help however I can. Because I am your mama."

She doesn't meet my gaze again; she just keeps smoothing the bags until I'm afraid she's going to start a fire from the friction.

"Okay. I hear you." After a few long beats of uncomfortable silence, my heart pounding heavily in my chest, I add, "And… thank you. I didn't know about all those vitamins and things. I do want to heal as fast as possible, so I appreciate you doing that research and shopping for me."

"You're welcome, sweetheart." She sniffs briefly and rearranges her features so they're as unruffled as the bags she flattened. "Maybe you can come for dinner this week? I'll get your dad to grill some fish."

"That'd be nice, but I'm working pretty long hours."

"Well, maybe next weekend, then."

I follow her to the front door on my crutches. Before exiting, she holds her arms out. "Can I give you a hug?"

"Sure, Mom. Anytime."

After I shift the crutches away from my sides, her arms encircle my ribcage to give me a good long squeeze. "Love you, Sully."

"Love you, too, Mom," I whisper, my throat tight. "See you soon."

# CHAPTER 13

> "Houston, we have a problem."
>
> –*Apollo 13*

## SULLY

WHENEVER I HAVE to skip out for PT during the day, I stay longer at the office. Helen hasn't ever given me a hard time for leaving in the middle of the day, but I can tell that the phone calls and emails pile up. Literally, there's a bigger pile on my desk when I return. If I don't stay to help take care of it, she just stays even later, and that's not fair. The woman's going to drive herself into an early grave the way she works.

Today, I also had a doctor's appointment, where I got a walking cast and the okay to change out the crutches for a cane. That was excellent news, but it also meant that I stayed even later tonight to get the work done.

As I enter Dani's house, the scent that greets me—something cheesy and meaty and Italian—is the only thing giving me the strength to drag my ass from the front door to the kitchen instead of diving headfirst into my bed.

"Did you cook for me again, girl?" I call. "I'm getting spoiled."

"Nope," she yells. "Your mama dropped this off. I just heated it up."

I find Dani in the kitchen finishing up her own dinner. "Sorry I didn't wait for you," she says with her mouth full. "But I was starving."

I glance at the kitchen clock as I scoop a large serving onto my plate. "It's later than I thought."

"Helen's working you hard, huh?"

"Yeah, but I need the money."

"Sorry to be the bearer of bad news, but it looks like you got some more bills today, as well as a very official-looking letter from some Virginia government place."

Bills can wait. I've taken to opening them all on Saturday and triaging them as best I can. But curiosity and dread has me opening the letter from the Virginia Marine Police, even as I stuff food into my mouth.

"Slow down. It ain't going anywhere. And I am not in the mood to perform the Heimlich this evening."

I just grunt in response, but I do my best to chew before swallowing. As I read through the pages, however, I put my fork down.

"What do they say?"

"A lot." The words begin to swim on the page as I try to take it all in. Instead of trying to summarize, I hand them over to Dani. "See for yourself."

As she reads, she mutters expletives in response. When she finishes, she carefully sets the papers on the counter like they might get up and run off. "Sounds like you need to take a trip to Virginia. And maybe get yourself a lawyer."

## HELEN

Just as it seemed as though things were settling into a routine where everyone in the production office has found their own rhythm, meaning that we operate as a well-oiled machine, ready to face any challenges thrown our way, Sully comes to work in a funk. By ten o'clock he's made three mistakes that'd have me yelling at any other PA, but I can tell he's not just being an idiot.

Something's wrong.

So I call him into my office. "Sit down and tell me what's going on."

Ignoring the order, he hovers in the doorway.

"For the love of god, Calloway. Would you just sit the hell down and put your damn foot up so I can concentrate?"

Grunting, he does as I ask. But then he just crosses his arms over his chest, his mouth in a grim line.

"What is going on?" I repeat.

"Nothing."

"Fuck you, Calloway."

He just blinks.

"You think I can't tell that something is bothering you? If that problem is affecting your work, then I need to know about it."

"Always back to the work."

"Well, yes. You are my assistant. And your mistakes reflect on me."

He just frowns.

"Wasting time here. Spit it out so we can fix it and move on."

"You can't fix everything, O'Neill."

"I sure as hell can try. I am a problem-solving genius, so lay it on me." Never in my life have I wanted to give a person a hug, but god help me, I do right now. To counteract that urge, I just get meaner. "What, are you embarrassed to tell me?"

"I am not embarrassed. I just don't think there's anything you can do."

Now it's my turn to simply wait until he breaks. No one can survive a Helen O'Neill stare down.

"Fine," he says on an irritated sigh. "My boat's been impounded up in Virginia while the accident was under investigation. That's over, so I have to go up there, pick up my belongings that've been stuck on board, and meet with the insurance adjuster, probably just to hear that they're totaling it."

"What does your lawyer say?"

"What lawyer?"

"You didn't hire representation?"

He frowns. "I hate lawyers."

"Pfft. Everyone does, until they need one."

Over the next fifteen minutes, I manage to drag Sully's story out of him—the one I told him I didn't need to hear the day I hired him. Apparently, he was the victim of the boating version of a hit-and-run and had been saved by local Good Samaritans who witnessed the accident. It'd taken all this time, but law enforcement had managed to find the culprits.

"What about damages?" I press.

He shrugs. "I was letting the insurance company deal with it."

"They're going to cover their asses. But you've suffered loss of work, and I'm sure you've got medical bills up the wazoo." I tap the eraser end of a pencil on my desk as I run through various ideas in my head.

"I did what the law required."

As I flip through my Rolodex, I shake my head. "You're not the one who broke it. Ah, here we are." Tucking the receiver into the crook of my neck, I begin to tap out the number for the lawyer we work with here in Wallington.

"You don't happen to have any of your paperwork with you, do you?"

"Just the letter I got from the marine police. I was going to call the insurance company today; I've just been putting it off."

Before I finish dialing, I shove a stack of paperwork across the desk.

"I'll trade you. While I make some phone calls, you can go over yesterday's time sheets, make copies for the union reports, and then get them to Dee. I'll see what I can turn up. I'm sure you're owed something."

As he struggles to his feet, he growls, "I can't pay a lawyer."

"You've been maimed, dude. I can't believe you haven't had personal injury lawyers knocking down your door." I wave him off. "I've got this. Get to work."

## SULLY

A week ago, it took me hours to process time sheets. Between the alphabet soup of unions—IATSE, SAG, DGA—each with its own forms and rules and paymasters and the moving target of a budget, it was a challenge to make sure that all the numbers went in all the right places.

From the day I started work, that was important to me. Not just because Helen would yell at me if I made a mistake. Which she did. But because I know firsthand how important it is that each person on the show has their hours reported correctly so they get the paycheck they're owed as well as the credit toward their health insurance.

Something else you don't really think about until you need it.

After I hand over the reports to Dee—and get a full

rundown on her son's health, which, thankfully, is all good—trading them for a stack of checks and different reports that Helen needs to sign off on, the phone rings.

"Who's this?" a familiar voice asks before I can say anything. "Hello? Can you hear me?"

"Zeke? It's Sully." The first AD sounds panicked, so when he doesn't answer, I summon patience. Wallington's cell coverage is notoriously non-existent, and calls drop in and out even when you can get through. "I'm still here. I'll hang on until you find a spot where you have service."

He's panting by the time his voice comes through again. "Yeah, sorry, Sully. I'm just a little—I mean, we've got a problem."

By the time he manages to fill me in on what happened, half of which I don't get because he keeps dropping out, all worries about me and my boat are shoved to the side. "What do you need from us?"

"I don't know, man. This has never happened to me before. I think Helen needs to get down here and make the call, but I don't think we can keep shooting without the director."

"Right. She's on the phone, but I'll get her to set stat."

"Thanks, man. I'll see you in a few."

After hanging up, I grab the call sheet and note the location. As fate would have it, they're shooting about as far away from the office as you could be and still be in Wallington, in some little house down off Masonboro Loop Road.

She hangs up the phone just as I arrive in the doorway.

"Good news," she begins. "I've got you an attorn—"

Holding up a hand, I interrupt her. "That's gonna have to wait. We've got a problem."

## HELEN

A unit production manager's job is all about problem-solving, but I've never had to deal with something on this scale. When your director—who according to the insurance-mandated pre-production doctor's visit has no major health concerns—collapses in the middle of a take, everything comes to a screeching halt.

Sully fills me in on what he knows on our way to the car, and I try to connect with the first AD on the drive there, but this town and its fucking lack of cell coverage makes that impossible. The minute we park, a PA sprints over, hands me a walkie, and then leads us to the production trailer. Inside, all of the crew chiefs are talking at once. Before I open my mouth to try to get their attention, Sully says, "Listen up" with just the right level of volume and authority to quiet the room instantly.

After a muttered thanks to him, I clear my throat. "Zeke, fill me in."

He quickly explains that Joe had said he wasn't feeling great when he arrived this morning, that he thought he might have eaten something off because he'd thrown up in the middle of the night. He'd asked the medic for Tums at some point because he was having some abdominal pain. But then halfway through a take, he'd doubled over in pain, and after a quick consult, the medic called 911.

"And?" I ask when he doesn't go on.

"We just heard from the second AD. She followed the ambulance to the hospital. Joe's having an emergency appendectomy."

"Jesus." I run a hand through my hair. "Okay. I guess that's good news in some ways. I mean, that's a pretty routine thing, right? How long will he be out?"

"From what she's learned, it depends. Could be one week, or it could be up to four."

Halting production for one week is expensive. Stopping it for four weeks is catastrophic. I take a deep breath in hope of finding an ounce of calm before scanning the faces before me. "Okay. Let's go over today's call sheet to see if there's anything we can get covered at this location without Joe. Exteriors, B-roll, that kind of thing. Once that's done, Zeke will call the day and send everyone home. In the meantime, I want that second AD calling my office with an update every hour."

Once we're back at the office, I call LA. It's still early there, so the executive producer isn't in yet, but I let the EP's assistant know that the director's in the hospital and that we'll need a conference call as soon as we have more information.

No more news from the hospital, so my next call is to the production insurance company. I need to gather as much information as possible before conferencing with the producers in California. I'd always thought insuring stars and other major players was a waste of money, but now it makes sense. We can't continue this production as planned without the director.

We also can't just tell the crew to wait around while he recovers without paying them. We'll have to lay people off so they can collect unemployment. Half of us are here from out of town and can't just be stranded. If we close down, do we fly everyone home or let them stay in their rentals? Or give them the choice? If we have to extend, we'll be paying rent on all the housing for an extra week, maybe even a month.

Creating a production budget and schedule is like putting a puzzle together. It's a Sisyphean task: every day some pieces of the puzzle get tossed, while others get reconfigured. Meaning, each day I have to do it all over again.

But this—it's like someone just put the puzzle pieces in a blender and then handed me back the shreds.

The numbers from insurance give me some relief, but we still have a lot of problem-solving to do. When Sully shows up with a large coffee and a pastry bag from Randy at craft service, I make grabby hands at him.

"Caffeine and sugar. Exactly what I need."

"Don't you want to know what it is?" Sully asks as he makes his way to my desk and sets both items down.

"I really don't care. I just need the fuel." When I open the bag, I get a waft of pure chocolate from the enormous muffin inside. Pulling off a bite, I shove it into my mouth. "Thank you."

"What else do you need, boss?"

I tick off a list. "Glenda. All of our housing contracts. Then I need to talk to union reps—SAG, IATSE 695, all the usual suspects. We need to know our options if production gets shut down for a week versus a month."

Sully pales. "Is that definitely what's going to happen?"

I point at him. "Don't be spreading any gossip, but yeah, shutting down is pretty much inevitable at this point. The only questions are: how long and what do we do with everyone in the meantime?"

"Oh, well, if those are the only questions…"

His sarcasm is, for once, not welcome.

"Yeah. Enough chat. Get Glenda's ass in here. She and I need to go into emergency mode."

As he turns to go, I notice something other than his very fine ass. "Hey. When did you lose the crutches?"

He looks down at the cane he's using instead. "Yesterday."

"Huh. Well, good for you, right?"

"Yep. Getting better. One day at a time."

"All right. Get outta here then."

# CHAPTER 14

"Do you like apples?"

"Yeah."

"Well, I got her number. How do you like them apples?"

—*Good Will Hunting*

## SULLY

IT TAKES two very long days for Helen and Glenda to shut down production. Since it apparently took them an entire month to get production ramped up, I suppose it could've been worse. I've been running errands and delivering messages and making calls as they work, a little in awe of how Helen manages to browbeat and cajole everyone from local landlords to union reps into giving us a break.

Long story short: the director's appendix burst and was septic, so he's out for at least two weeks, possibly four. Helen's wheeling and dealing has made it so every out-of-town cast and crew member has the choice to stay here in rental housing or fly home for the shutdown. Everyone gets laid off, even the department heads, which is apparently unheard of. There are a few hiccups with actor schedules, but between the Thanksgiving and Christmas holidays, hardly anyone had a job set up right after this one, so we catch a break that way.

For me personally, the good news/bad news is: I now have time to fetch my boat.

Good news because it needs to get done.

Bad news because I'm not sure I can face it.

"So, we're done?" I ask Helen after she sends both John and Dee home Thursday afternoon. "Done, done?"

She looks around the quiet office. "Done, done. You can go home, and I'll… see you later."

A groan escapes from my mouth.

Helen gives me a sharp look. "What's the matter? I thought you were getting better?"

I shake my head. "It's not my leg. I just have to go get my boat out of impound."

"I guess that won't exactly be a fun trip." She rubs her forehead with a thumb and forefinger. "Shit. I forgot all about the lawyer."

I wave that down. "Don't worry about it."

"I have it in here." She disappears into her office, emerging a few moments later with a message slip. "Our Wallington lawyer recommends this guy up in Virginia. Guess he's a real bulldog."

I take the slip and shove it into my pocket. I'm not going to use it, but I don't say so since she made the effort. "Thanks. Uh, I guess I'll see you in a couple weeks."

"You're going up there by yourself?"

I shrug in answer.

"How long a drive is it to get there?"

"Uh…" I scratch the back of my neck. "About five hours, I think."

"Is that a good idea? With your injury?"

I shrug again. "It's fine. I'm not going to sail the boat back. Neither one of us is seaworthy."

"What about your friends? Can't Dani or someone go with you?"

"Nah. They all have to work."

"Anybody else? Your family?"

"It's the school year, so they have to work too. My parents teach at the university."

"Well, then." She sets her hands on her hips and looks off to the side. "I don't know why I'm saying this, but I will go with you if you want."

"What?" Surprise has me stumbling backward and tangling with my desk chair. Even as my entire body screams *YES*, once I get my balance, I say, "No, you're not."

"You can't tell me what to do." She gestures at me. "Plus, look at you. You can't make a five-hour drive all by yourself. You can barely stand."

"I'm a lot better. It's really not—"

"If I don't go, I'll be stuck here all twitchy with nothing to do."

"You could take a vacation."

She nods sharply. "If it were the end of production, I would. But it's not."

"You don't have to go anywhere. You can have margaritas on the beach with Glenda and Sherry and Kara and them."

"Everyone who's not from here is going back to LA. Except Glenda, but her husband's coming here. I am not going to be their third wheel." She crosses her arms and nods like it's all settled. "Anyway, I'm in project mode."

It's my turn to tick a finger back and forth in the air. A gesture I've borrowed from my boss. "I. Am not. Your project."

Although she's probably right that the trip will be a hell of a lot easier with another person to drive and help me get everything off the boat, so much could go wrong. Including her regretting everything from traveling with me to hiring me. "Not only that, there're no five-star hotels where I'm going. There aren't even hotels—just motels. It's the middle of nowhere. Every fish is fried."

She looks out the window. "I thought this was the middle of nowhere."

"You're such a city girl."

"I'm kidding. Look, I've shot in the sticks before. I've slept in motels and eaten in crappy diners." She rubs her hands together, an almost gleeful expression on her face. "Mm, mm, mmm. I'll bet there will be some problem-solving to be done. You know I'm good at that. And seriously…" She walks into her office, still talking. "If you go up there by yourself, I'll just worry the whole time. It's a win-win."

She exits her office, turns off the light, and locks the door, but I still haven't agreed to her cockamamie plan, so she goes for the big guns. She gives me that stare. The one where, if she were a cat, her tail would be twitching. "Limited time offer," she sing-songs.

When I finally close my eyes and nod, she actually claps.

"So when do we leave?"

## HELEN

After I leave the office and go back to my apartment, after I've somehow and for some unknown-to-me reason convinced Sully to take me to Virginia with him, I'm too restless to settle down, so I spend the evening cleaning the rental, arguing with myself the entire time.

As I vacuum, I mutter, "What do you think this is, O'Neill? A rom-com? If you're lucky, it's a road trip movie."

As I collect newspapers and toss them into the recycling, I reason that he's a big guy. It's not like I can physically overpower him and make him have sex with me. If it happened, it would be totally consensual.

But when I picture his face as I Windex the bathroom mirror, I have to admit that he's practically a kid, a young guy in an emotionally vulnerable situation. Therefore, I can and should keep my hands off of him.

Then, filling the dishwasher, a little movie plays through my mind: Sully's back and arms flexing as he lifts a box into his lap. Which has me wishing he'd do the same to me.

*For fuck's sake, Helen, admit it.* Even a nun would think twice about ditching her vows, given the opportunity to get jiggy with Sullivan Calloway.

Pulling clothes out of the dryer, I remind myself that I do have a very good reason for offering to go. He is injured and can use the extra set of hands and legs. As well as an extra problem-solving brain.

But as I shove clothes into an overnight bag—bathing suit: yes or no? Pajamas: yes or no? Sexy underwear: yes or no?—I have to concede that every choice I make is evidence that I plan on seducing him.

Finally, when I drop the bagged trash in the outside bin, I conclude that sleeping with him would be okay because he's not my employee for the next two weeks.

In bed, I lie awake wondering if his skin is that lovely golden brown everywhere. When I finally fall asleep, my dreams are rated triple-X. They're so dirty, and I'm so turned on the next morning I call him a half hour before we're supposed to meet. But instead of backing out—the sensible thing to do—I convince him to take my rental car. With me in it. After all, there's more space for him to stretch out, and I've got unlimited mileage, so why put the wear and tear on his car?

Minutes later, I pull up in front of his house and beep the horn. No way I'm going inside. If Dani sees my face, she'll know what I'm thinking. When he emerges from the front door to hobble down the front walk, a bag slung over his broad shoulders, I pop the trunk and roll down the windows, but I don't get out.

Surprisingly, he gets into the passenger seat without argument.

"You're okay with me driving?"

"Your name's on the contract." He unfolds a combination Virginia / North Carolina map. "I'll navigate."

"Don't you know how to get there already?"

"Not exactly," he says as he refolds the map revealing a route that he's highlighted with pink marker. Adorable.

"But you've been there before."

"Sort of, and only by boat. The marine police office is about twenty miles from the creek I was anchored in." He squints at the map. "There's no easy way to get to eastern Virginia from here by car. Except for the new extension of this interstate"—his finger traces the route—"all the highways are two-lane roads with no bypasses, so you have to slow down to go through every little town."

After he gives me the initial directions and I pull away from the curb, I ask, "So, if it's such a pain in the ass to get there, why take your boat?"

He relaxes into his seat, and the smile on his face is all the answer I need. "The Chesapeake Bay. Every captain I met who came through Wallington on his way up or down the intracoastal waterway told me it's the best sailing on the east coast. Big enough that you've got tons of places to explore, but small enough that you can anchor every night. It's hard to solo out on the Atlantic because you can't really sleep in the open ocean. I've wanted to go for years."

As he talks, his voice shifts from boyish excitement to something more somber. When I glance over, he's looking out the window so I can't see his expression, but I decide to change the subject. No need to drag him through grief he's probably still processing, so I change tack. "So, did you always want to be a cable guy?"

"Nice segue," he says, but there's a chuckle, so I ignore the jab. "But no. First off, when I was a teen, a cable guy was the guy who made it so you could watch TV."

"They had cable TV when you were a kid?"

"We didn't until I was in high school because my parents are culture snobs. But Violet's grandparents got it at their inn when we were in junior high."

"Huh." I try to figure out the math. I didn't get cable until I was in my twenties. "How old are you, anyway?"

"Twenty-eight. How old are you?"

"You're not supposed to ask a woman's age."

"But you just asked mine."

"It's different."

"That's pretty sexist."

"Fine. I'm thirty-eight."

"Wow. I thought you were older."

"For Christ's sake, Calloway."

"No"—he whacks himself in the forehead—"I don't mean you *look* old. Sorry. It's just, you're pretty high up the food chain. And you have your shit together."

"Hmph. I guess you're forgiven then." Since I really don't want to know how old he thinks I look, I circle back to my original question. "If you didn't want to be a cable guy like Jim Carrey, what did you want to be?"

"You saw that movie?"

"Sure. I see a lot of movies. When I'm not working."

"Huh."

"What?"

"I just didn't think you'd be a Jim Carrey fan."

"Why not?"

"You know. I thought you'd be more into, like, I don't know… *Wings of the Dove* or *The English Patient*."

"Snooty British films with stiff titles? Really? Why would you think that?"

"Because you seem classy like that."

I bark out a laugh. "You have got me all wrong. I told you I was born in New York, but I wasn't raised in a Park Place penthouse. I lived in a walkup in Queens."

He shrugs. "All the same to me. I've never been to New York City. So, did you want to be a UPM when you grew up?"

"Nobody thinks 'I want to be a UPM when I grow up.' It's the least sexy job on the call sheet."

"Well, producer then."

"I wanted to make movies. They were always an escape for me. My first job was at a movie theater." I swing a glance in his direction. "I was twelve."

"You got a job when you were twelve?"

"Yup. Told 'em I was fourteen. They didn't give a shit. They basically paid me in popcorn and hotdogs and soda. And movies."

"Did you study film in college?"

"Didn't go to college. Didn't have money for it. I just worked." I glance over again to gauge his reaction. People tend to get judgy when I say I skipped college. But he just looks thoughtful, his gaze out the window. "You ever going to tell me what you wanted to be when you grow up?"

He turns to face me, and his smile glows so bright I'm glad I have the excuse of driving to look away.

"I wanted to be a professional surfer."

"Is that a thing?"

"It is if you're good enough. But I was never good enough. I don't have the best physique for it."

I have to clamp my lips together to avoid saying anything about said physique.

"And then I wanted to be a marine biologist, but chemistry class was my downfall."

"How in the world did you end up working in production sound?"

"Not on purpose, that's for sure." He shifts, moving his seat back and adjusting the position of his leg. Just when I think he's not going to continue, he says, "My friend Ford got a job on a movie right after graduation. The right way. You know, do an internship, follow up with letters, get the offer. Me? I drove across the country with him on a whim and basically rode his coattails."

"Good way to get out of a small town, though."

"It wasn't that I *wanted* out. It was that I thought I *needed* to go. I hadn't really been anywhere else, and it seemed like a good opportunity to see another part of the country. Also, I was afraid that I'd lose my best friends if I stayed." He clears his throat. "Ford and I got into a fight over this girl Whitney, and that kind of tore the group into pieces."

"Whitney who does hair?"

"You know her?"

"I think so. Petite blonde with enormous blue eyes?"

"That's her."

"She worked on the other movie I did in Wallington. Gave a decent haircut too."

"Decent?" he says, his tone defensive. "She's really good."

"To me, 'decent' is high praise." I slide an appraising look his way and decide to be direct. "You were in love with her?"

He hesitates before answering. "I don't think so, not really. Pretty sure it was more about me and Ford, to be honest. I didn't get that at the time, of course."

"Wait, so you were fighting with this guy over a girl, but you moved across the country with him anyway?"

"It was his idea for me to go with him, and I couldn't say no. Ford, me, Dani, who you know"—he catches my eye, and I nod—"and Violet and Whitney, we've all known each other since we were little. Stayed friends all the way through college. The girls were mad that we left at first. So was Mr. Jones."

"Who's Mr. Jones?"

"Mr. Jones is my cat. Or he was. Oh, shit. You need to get off here."

I'm going over seventy, and after quickly scanning the traffic surrounding us, I decide it's not worth the risk to try to make the ramp. "Too late. We'll have to turn around at the next exit. I wouldn't mind stopping, anyway."

Unfortunately, the next exit is ten miles down the road, and then we have to travel several miles to find a gas station. As I pull in, Sully says he'll fill the tank and insists on paying for it. While he does that, I brave the public restroom.

When I return to the car, he's studying the map. "I found a different route so we don't have to double back."

"Great. I got us nourishment so we won't starve."

Sully laughs when he sees my purchases. "RC Cola and corn nuts?"

"It's what the guy ahead of me was getting." I shrug. "When in Rome, right?"

"Whatever you say, *boss*."

He gives the word a teasing tone that makes me want to show him exactly who's the boss in the most fundamental way. Instead, as I slide into the driver's seat, I just say, "Remember, we're laid off. I'm not your boss right now."

There's undeniable heat in his eyes as they drop to my lips. Enough to get me revved up, but no way am I making out with this guy in a gas station parking lot on the side of the country road, so I carefully insert the key into the lock and ignite the car's engine.

Once we're on the way and I've calmed down a bit, I remember the last thing he said before we missed the exit. "Wait. So, what happened to your cat?"

## SULLY

After I answer Helen's questions about Mr. Jones, my mood takes a dive. It's obviously the stupidest idea in the world to have brought Helen along. Not only have I got a Gordian knot of feelings for her—feelings that get more intense the more I learn about her—but the closer we get to the bay and my boat, the tighter the coil in my gut. I don't want to fall apart in front of my boss, but I'm not sure if I'll be able to keep it from happening.

I'd really like to just take a nap and forget it all, but I don't want to miss another exit. To stay awake without descending into a funk, I need mindless distraction. "Mind if I turn on the radio?"

"Sure."

Even though I search both AM and FM dials, the stations are few and far between.

Helen punches the off button when I hit static for the fortieth or fiftieth time. "I can't listen to that or country music or some guy talking about Jesus."

"Yeah, not my cup of tea either."

Then I remember that I had the good sense to grab my music collection from my car before we left this morning. "Luckily, I brought my stash."

"Of marijuana?" she asks, almost hopefully.

"Uh, no. I haven't smoked for a few years now."

"Yeah, me neither." Her sigh sounds wistful, but I'm not going to press her on that.

"I meant music."

"As long as it isn't country or soft rock"—she shudders—"I'm good."

"Oh, man." I slap a palm to my forehead, pulling out the stops on the overacting. "I was going to put in Seals and Crofts. Maybe John Denver or The Carpenters instead?"

"Gah. That's the kind of crap my mother used to listen to."

"Don't you worry your pretty little head." I hold up the new CD mix I made last weekend to rotate out with the one Ford made. "This has got all the good stuff on it. Not just

Pearl Jam, but a couple of Blind Melon songs, Stone Temple Pilots—"

She jabs a finger at the radio. "Enough yammering. Put it in already."

I literally have to bite my tongue to keep from acknowledging the sexual innuendo. *Not going there.*

As our heads bob in time to the music and the car glides along the empty highway, I can't stop thinking about the fact that, despite differences in ages and geography, Helen and I have a hell of a lot in common.

All the reasons why we shouldn't act on the sexual tension zinging between us—like that moment back in that gas station parking lot—start to seem kind of dumb. A little out-of-town fling could be just what we need.

It'd be a risk.

To my job as well as my heart.

But it might be worth it.

# CHAPTER 15

"Quitting is not going to make you stronger. Living will."

–*Pump Up the Volume*

## HELEN

"I KNOW WE'RE ALMOST THERE," I say a few hours later, after we turn onto a cracked and dusty lane that makes the country road we left behind seem like a major highway. "But I've got to eat. Could we stop for lunch before we go to wherever we're going?"

"The Gloucester Field Office of the Virginia Marine Police," Sully says over a yawn, stretching his arms overhead to the point that his T-shirt rides up, exposing muscular abs and the happiest of happy trails. When he pats that flat belly with a groan, I peel my eyeballs away so forcefully my hands wobble.

He reaches over to steady the steering wheel. "You okay?"

"Yeah, just hungry." *For more than simple calories.*

He releases the wheel and checks his watch. "We can stop. It's only two, and I'm pretty sure they're open until five."

Fifteen minutes of tobacco field-lined so-called highway

later, I pull into the gravel lot of a place that looks like it hasn't had an update since 1929. But the parking lot is full, and my stomach is growling.

"Locals seem to like it," Sully says, echoing my thoughts.

Inside, a waitress with a thick accent tells us to sit wherever we want, and a few minutes later, she drops two sticky single-page menus on the table. "Welcome to Joe's. What kind of coke do you want, honey?"

"What kind of coke?"

She just nods and smiles.

"What kind of coke do you have?" I ask slowly.

"We got Coke, Diet Coke, Sprite, Orange, and iced tea."

"Oh, okay. Can I just have water?"

"You can, but you won't like it." She winces. "It's well water."

"Got it. I'll have tea, then."

"It's going to be sweet, Helen," Sully warns.

When I ask for tea without sugar, the waitress looks even more displeased. "You want *un*sweet?"

"Yes?" I do my best not to make my answer a question, but even I am thrown by the look on her face, like she's been told the customer's always right, but she firmly disagrees. When I don't change my order, her nostrils remain flared as she turns to Sully. "How about you, sir?"

Sully orders a Coke and asks what her favorite thing on the menu is. When she immediately answers the crab cake sandwich, we both order that.

"It comes with one vegetable." She points at the list of sides, very few of which seem to actually be vegetables. I choose the green beans, and Sully gets fried okra.

I excuse myself, and by the time I get back from the bathroom, the food is waiting. "That was fast."

Sully waits for me to sit before digging in, but I don't hesitate to take a bite. "Oh my god, this is good."

"Seriously good."

I examine the crab cake's interior. "This thing is all crab. Hardly any filler. It's not fried, either."

"It's not *deep* fried. But the okra is," he adds before popping one into his mouth.

"The beans aren't, but"—I spear a flaccid object from the bowl the waitress delivered—"they're not exactly green."

He peers at the small ceramic dish. "Yeah. Overcooked. With bacon, probably."

I drop the bean, opting to take another bite of my sandwich. "I don't care. This is the best fucking thing I've eaten all year."

He laughs and shakes his head, dropping his gaze. Which is a good thing. Now that I've started to entertain the possibility of sleeping with him, too much eye contact might make me spontaneously combust.

## SULLY

I'm still thinking about the look of rapture on Helen's face when she bit into that sandwich—and wondering if I know any moves that'd recreate it—when we arrive at the Marine Police Operations center.

As Helen pulls into the driveway leading to an unremarkable pale-yellow building, I crane my neck and search the boat yard behind it, both dreading and dying to see *Endless Summer*.

"This seems to be the place." Helen puts the car in park and turns off the engine. "What now?"

"I guess we go inside."

When I unfasten my seatbelt but don't make a move to exit, Helen reaches over and gives my forearm a quick squeeze. "Rip off the Band-Aid?"

Bile rises, making me regret the fried okra, but I swallow it back and nod. "You coming in?"

"Hmm. I am tempted to go get a shampoo and set, see how big a bouffant they can create." She tips her chin at the bright pink stucco building next door, punningly called Anita Haircut, before pointing at the building on the other side. "Or, if you want to go fishing after, I can pick us up some bait at Hooked Up."

I shake my head, but her goofy expression and out-of-character joking have me laughing. As I grab my cane and exit the car, I catch her eye. "Thanks for the distraction."

"I don't know what you're talking about." She falls in on my right side since I'm using the cane on my left. "I've always wondered what I'd look like with a blue rinse."

I'm still chuckling as we step inside, but when I catch sight of a man in the same uniform as the guy that had visited my hospital room right after the accident, the jokes get left at the door. That marine cop had only bad news for me; this time it'll probably be worse.

"Can I help y'all?" asks a woman with an eastern Virginia drawl.

I hold up the letter I received. "Uh, yeah. I'm here to see Officer Davis."

She asks my name and then points to a few benches in the small waiting area. "I'll tell him you're here."

Instead of sitting, I hobble over to examine a large framed map of the Chesapeake Bay.

"Wow. That's a lot of squiggles." Helen's finger traces the bay's boundary lines and tributaries.

"This doesn't even show the half of it. In real life, every single one of those squiggles has smaller waterways running off of it, little creeks and rills."

"Can you sail them all?"

"Not all. Most aren't deep enough." I lead her to another framed picture, an illustration of the various types of boating vessels. "What's the main difference between the power boats and the sailboats?"

She snorts. "You mean besides the sail and the motor?"

I point to the motor at the stern of a sailboat. "Many sail-boats actually have motors, for when the wind dies. But yes, besides that."

She points to a keel. "Are you talking about this thingy?"

"Yep. That thingy, called the keel, means that a sailboat has a deeper draw. Which means I can't go as many places as a powerboat."

"Why not use a powerboat then?"

"Maybe I can show you why sometime."

O'Neill's chin lifts, as if she's about to meet my challenge with one of her own, but before she gets a word out, a male voice calls, "Sullivan Calloway?"

"Got to face the music," I mutter before facing the officer. "That's me, sir."

## HELEN

There's a whole lot of something zinging back and forth between me and Mr. Calloway, but before I can call him on it, he gets ushered in to speak to one of the boat cops.

I believe I've done an excellent job of distracting Sully from his obvious discomfort at returning to the scene of his accident, but now *my* thoughts need some redirection. Because they've created an entire scene in Sensurround with me and Sully at the wheel of a sailboat, the wind in our hair, and "My Heart Will Go On" in the background.

Clearly, I need to get a grip.

Anyway, unlike Jack and Rose, we aren't sleeping on a boat tonight. On the drive up, Sully confessed that he hadn't made a reservation, so I decide to use the wait to find us a place to stay.

My cell phone has no bars—big surprise. There's a payphone in the corner, but the little chain that normally anchors the yellow pages hangs empty, so I ask the receptionist if I can borrow one.

"Y'all here for the Crab Fest?" she asks as she pulls a directory out of a desk drawer.

"Oh, no. We're just here to see about his boat. Any suggestions for places to stay?"

"Y'all don't have a reservation?" When I shake my head, she winces. "'Cause of the festival, there ain't gonna be much anywhere nearby."

Glancing at my watch, I calculate how late we'd get back to Wallington if we leave before dark. It'd be the wee hours, but that might be better than staying in some crappy motel on the side of the highway. If we could even find one.

"Except"—the woman lengthens the vowels of the word as she picks up the phone—"my cousin works at the Visitors' Center. I'll see if she knows about any last-minute cancellations."

"Oh, you don't have to—"

"It's no trouble—oh, hey, Gina. Listen, I've got a lady here looking for a room for tonight... I know I told her everything'd be booked up but—uh-huh..."

As she yammers on to her cousin, I try to decide whether to tell her that we'd need two rooms, but I'm not even certain of the answer myself. I think Sully's been sending signals of interest, but I could be deluding myself.

"Okay, let me ask," the woman says. "She found a cabin available, but there's a three-night minimum."

"A cabin?"

"It's in this real cute little resort on the Piankatank River. Right off Route 3, but it's quiet." She waggles her eyebrows. "Romantic."

I rarely blush, but my cheeks are currently in three-alarm-fire mode. If this woman can sense the sexual tension between Sully and me, then maybe I'm not creating it out of thin air. I should say, "No thank you, ma'am, we'll just head on back to North Carolina," but instead I say, "We'll take it."

After she gives her cousin my name, she hangs up and writes down the details about our reservation. As she slides the piece of paper across her desk, she winks. "You go, girl."

I take it, my face still blazing. "Thanks. I will… do that."

# CHAPTER 16

"I figure life's a gift and I don't intend on wasting it. You never know what hand you're gonna get dealt next. You learn to take life as it comes at you. To make each day count."

—*Titanic*

## HELEN

WHEN I STEP out into the parking lot, the slight chill in the air doesn't do much to cool me down. My imagination is firing on all cylinders, turning heated moments between Sully and me from the past few weeks into an NC-17 rated movie that I can't wait to bring to life.

Even though I said I didn't want to, even though it'd be breaking my rules, even though it's likely a bad idea, sex with Sully is all I can think about.

I've waded so deep into the fantasy I don't even take in the uniformed officer brushing past me. "Excuse me, ma'am."

Realizing that he's the man Sully was meeting with, I call out. "Um, sorry. Is Mr. Calloway still here?"

The officer turns but continues to walk backward as he

speaks. "I've got to respond to an emergency, but yes"—he points to a spot somewhere behind me—"he's still aboard."

He jogs off and is joined in the parking lot by a few other officers, who all jump into various vehicles and drive off, sirens blaring.

When I turn back to the sea of boats—each and every one suspended above ground so they look like they're floating in the air—I'm glad I have a few clues to help me narrow down the options. I just learned that only the sailboats have the keel thingy dangling below and on the ride up, Sully told me his is named after a movie. I can't remember which one, so I work my way through the sailing vessels, reading the names painted on their rear ends.

*Knotty Girl. Seas the Day. New Kid on the Dock.*

Yowza. Boating people must love ban puns as much as beauty salon owners.

After I round the corner of a very large boat called *In Too Deep*, I spy a sailboat with the name *Endless Summer*.

Ding-ding-ding: *Endless Summer* was a classic surfer documentary from the sixties. He's too young to have seen that, but then I remember that they made a follow up in 1994. Just as a smile lifts the corners of my mouth, it's frozen by a sound coming from the boat.

A roar of pain.

The tripods holding *Endless Summer* off the ground don't look stable enough to keep her from tipping, but that doesn't stop me from climbing the steps of a ladder leading to the back of the boat, scrambling into the well that holds the big steering wheel, and rushing toward the wrenching sounds of Sully's anguish.

I hesitate at the top of the steps leading down into the room below deck. "Sully?"

The sound of a clogged throat clearing precedes his answer. "I'm here."

"Is everything okay? I mean, are you hurt?"

My eyes have adjusted to the relatively dim light enough that I can see him shift to sitting upright and wipe his face with the sleeve of his T-shirt. "Yeah. I'm—I'm not… injured."

"Can I come inside?"

Several long seconds pass before he says, "Sure."

I creep down the stairs, unreasonably worried the boat will tip over, to find him seated on an upholstered bench on one side of the cabin. The space is tiny, but cabinets made of beautifully burnished wood line the interior. There's even a little kitchen and what looks like a mini bedroom. It doesn't seem damaged, until I really look at the side Sully's facing. The cabinet on that side is bowed, the wood is cracked, and its doors hang off-kilter.

He seems to be staring blindly into space, so I sit down next to him on the little couch. "Was the news bad?"

Lips pressed together, he shrugs and shakes his head, obviously holding back emotion.

I suck at making people feel better. Big emotions are not my forte, so my mind spins. I know nothing about boats, but I do know how to deal with lawyers and insurance brokers and contractors. Hell, I spent last week wheedling shit out of the movie's insurance company.

But as I try to figure out what to say or do, nothing seems right. Then, without direction from my brain, my arm reaches across his broad back, and I pull him close. He resists for half a second before crumpling sideways to rest his cheek on my shoulder. My hand rubs his back as his ribs expand and contract. Heaving at first and then stuttering, and then evening out.

I'm not sure how long we sit pressed against each other, the only sounds his breath and the clinking of boat things in the light wind. When his arm snakes around my waist and his lips find the skin of my neck, it's clear that desire has replaced grief.

Finally, a feeling I know what to do with.

## SULLY

I know I should ask permission, but I'm afraid if I speak, I'll fall apart. Trusting that Helen's a woman who knows her own mind—I can't imagine anyone making her do anything she doesn't want to—I let my lips and hands speak for me and hope against hope hers will answer in kind.

"I've been dying to know what you taste like," she whispers as her lips find my brow.

She's a cocktail my mouth can't get enough of. Something tart, something sweet. When I slide a hand under her shirt, she shivers as my fingers skate over soft skin covering taut muscles, but her moan gives me permission to continue my exploration.

"C'mere," is the most I can say, my voice rough from a swell of emotion.

"Your leg," she whispers. "Is it—"

In answer, I slip one hand under her butt and lift her onto my lap so she's straddling me. After adjusting her seat so that the neediest part of me is pressed into her cleft, I slide my hand from one set of cheeks to the other.

Once I've captured her face, I grip it gently but firmly. "I need you."

"Here?" Her gaze darts toward the light streaming into the cabin from the cockpit. "Now?"

With a finger to her chin, I guide her eyes back to mine. "Right here. Right now."

Eyes widen and nostrils flare, but she nods. "You got a condom, *boss*, you're on."

When I grin at her playful use of the word, she just grinds into me.

Thankfully, the box of Trojans I'd optimistically stowed when I outfitted my boat isn't in the busted cabinet, so it's likely still intact. Grappling blindly behind me until I find it, I rip the top off the box and then dump the contents onto the divan next to me.

"Got plenty of 'em," I growl.

She levers back and glances around the interior. "This thing stable?"

"'Sfar as I know. Not exactly private, though."

She glances at the cabin entrance again before granting me a sly smile. "Cops all left to deal with some emergency. Turns out you've got me all to yourself. As long as Darla stays in the office, that is."

"That's a risk I'm willing to take." Spearing fingers through her short hair, I zero in on the mouth I've been fantasizing about, tipping her head at the last minute to angle my kiss. At contact, I light up like an Operation game, flashing lights zinging from lips to balls, a live wire that I don't want to run to ground.

Her mouth parts with a whine, and my tongue paints her lips with hunger that won't be sated. Teeth want in, too. Nipping, sucking, biting, each eliciting deeper sighs and moans that resonate from her shuddering flesh to mine.

As my hands knead and caress her slim frame, her hips begin to roll with urgency. My hands fumble with the buttons of her shirt and she does the same with mine. After freeing her breasts, my palms delight in their heft and softness, contrasting with the pebbled buds of her nipples between my thumbs and forefingers.

But it's not enough. I need to be inside this woman more than I need my next breath. I didn't think to ask the orthopedic surgeon whether or how I could have sex, but I am determined to make this work.

"Hang on," I rasp. "Clothes. Off."

"Uh-huh" is her panted answer. She scrambles off my lap and shucks her pants and thong; I balance on my right leg and shove my shorts and boxers down. I manage to fully extract the healthy leg before she's back on my lap, rubbing up and down my shaft and bringing my hands back to her breasts.

When she meets my gaze, her smile is glorious. "Ready to fuck me?"

I shake my head even as I grab a condom and rip the package open with my teeth. After I reach between us to roll it over my length, I seek out her heated center with two fingers, watching her eyes roll back and her lips part as my thumb circles. "Boss, I'm ready for *you* to fuck *me*."

## HELEN

Back at the office, I'm the boss.

Here and now, his words are my command.

So I do what he says.

I've got the Niagara Falls of juices flowing, so when I rise up and guide him home, he slides right in. Not that there's plenty of room. Just as the man's giant hands and feet promised, he makes for a tight fit, stretching me in the best way possible, the friction igniting nerves that send messages rippling out in every direction.

Rising and falling, I revel in the way he fills me up, but it's hard for me to come from internal stimulation alone, so when his palms grip my ass, I hold on to one shoulder for balance and reach between us to prime my engine. Middle finger massaging until a sweet heat begins to pulse, I'm close to letting go when he hisses "Yes" and begins to pound into me. I hang on for the ride, squeezing him tightly with my inner walls until a wave of pure pleasure breaks, and we collapse into each other, gasping to reclaim breath.

It's only when I open my eyes to bright sunlight that I

crash back to reality. We just had off-the-chain loud sex, basically outside.

"Oh, man, I hope Darla didn't go outside for a smoke in the middle of that." Just the image of her face has a giggle sneaking past my lips.

Sully snorts. "Pretty sure we just scared the wildlife for miles around."

Picturing the stampede has me laughing harder.

"All right, woman," Sully says with a light slap to my ass. "Glad to have been so entertaining."

His tone is mock gruff, his mood far lighter than it was when I stepped inside the dim cabin. After lifting me off his lap, he limps to a cabinet and reaches inside, giving me a view of his very fine ass. When he turns and pitches a towel at me, his smile is wide, and his eyes are clear.

"Let's clean up and get dressed before the cops get back."

# CHAPTER 17

"The seed of suffering in you may be strong, but don't wait until you have no more suffering before allowing yourself to be happy."

—Thich Nhat Hanh, *The Heart of the Buddha's Teaching*

## SULLY

"SO... I'd like to do that again, maybe in a bed," I say, after I stuff our used towels into a garbage bag. "Definitely taking my time. But I gotta pack up this stuff."

"Let's do it then."

Helen doesn't seem to regret the sexual encounter we just shared. In fact, by the look of wicked glee in her eye, the prospect of a repeat may have her working double-time.

As we move kitchenware, bedding, and maps into bags and boxes, I tell her everything I learned about the boat's status. "Good news is, the marine police have loads of evidence IDing the captain and are pretty sure he was intoxicated. Bad news is, they have no solid proof of the latter."

"But will he have to pay to fix your boat?" She eyes the crack in the hull. "And is it fixable?"

Tracing a finger along the splintered wood, I say,

"According to the police officer, that all gets worked out between the marine insurance people. I have to meet my agent Monday to make it official, but I guess it's not as damaged as I thought it was."

"And the other guy pays for it?"

"They go after the other guy's insurance, but yeah, basically." I don't need to bore her with all the details, but I add, "Fiberglass hulls have a lot of give. It caved in but then popped right back out, which meant less water damage."

"But"—a line forms between her eyebrows—"you seemed pretty upset before we… uh. You know."

Not wanting to return to the grief and rage and frustration I'd been feeling earlier, I just nod. "It's a lot, just seeing it, I guess."

She doesn't push for more, but once we've stowed the boxes and bags in the back of her rental, I reach for her.

"Need me to hold you up?" she asks with what almost passes for a shy smile.

"I need a hug, if that's okay."

She looks dubious even as she steps into my arms, but after a few beats, she hugs me back. We just stand there, holding on to each other for a long time. Eventually, she sort of pats me on the back and steps away.

Digging car keys out of her bag, she asks, "Shall we?"

"We still have to find a place to stay," I remind her as she pulls out of the driveway.

"I've got it covered." She hands me a piece of paper. "You navigate."

Fifteen minutes later, a sign for the Cozy Cove Resort appears.

"Only you could find a resort in the boondocks, O'Neill."

"I have my ways," she says with a grin. "Besides, I think the label 'resort' is stretching it here. Hang on, I'll get the key."

Before I can argue that I'll go with her and that I should

pay because she's helping me out, she's exited the car. Suddenly exhausted, I let my head fall back against the headrest. What a rollercoaster this afternoon has been.

Seeing the boat I'd lovingly restored with an ugly gash in her side was pretty upsetting, to say the least.

Then, when the officer told me it was likely that it'd be repaired, my heart soared.

But as I sat in the cabin, with my leg on the mend and *Endless Summer*'s future hopeful, the fact that Mr. Jones didn't make it hit me like a ton of bricks.

Then Helen walked in, and I'm not sure what the fuck happened. All I know is that, despite the grief still dogging me, I want to do it again. If she'll let me.

She's all bustling efficiency when she returns to the car with a set of keys and a map showing the layout of the wooded property. During the short drive to a cabin she rented for the weekend, which turns out to be beautifully situated with its own dock leading down to the river, she tells me all about the dinner she's ordered. "They'll bring it right to the room," she adds as she parks the car.

When she opens the door and ushers me inside the rustically—but from what I can tell, expensively appointed—rooms, I have to stop and take stock. "Helen. How much did this cost?"

She waves my question away. "Don't worry about it."

"I don't feel comfortable with you paying for this."

"Did you know there's a festival in town?"

"A festival?"

"It's Crab Feast or Fest or something like that, meaning there were no rooms at any inns. But Darla called her cousin and found us this."

Dropping my overnight bag on the floor, I take a quick tour of the place. It's super nice, but it is small. Returning to the main room, I ask, "You reserved this place *before* you found me in my boat?"

She bites her lip, then nods.

"Did you know there was only one bed?"

"I plead the fifth."

I shake my head. "You're gonna make me crazy."

She steps close and brushes her thumb across my lower lip. "I'd like to try."

Dropping my cane, I snag her hand and suck that thumb into my mouth, eliciting a moan of pleasure. When I drag it along my teeth, she grabs my ass with her free hand and presses her chest to mine. "Let's go get naked."

After removing her thumb from my mouth with a pop, I stroke both hands down her sides. "If I could pick you up and carry you to that bed, I would."

"Race you there," she whispers, before tapping the center of my chest, running the short distance to the bedroom and catapulting onto the bed before I make it through the doorway.

By the time I've removed my shirt, she's down to a sexy set of underwear I'd barely noticed in the dim light of the boat's interior. She turns on her side and watches hungrily as I drop my shorts.

"Dang it," I say, adding a sigh to my act.

"You okay?"

"Yeah, I just… really need to do my PT."

Her face falls. "Oh. Well. Sure. You should… do that."

"Thing is"—I shake my head with a wince—"I need a partner. To work my… hip flexors." Try as I may, I can't keep a straight face.

She throws a pillow at me. "You are mean."

Managing to snag it without losing my balance, I chuck it back at her, gasping in mock affront. "I'm serious. I need a very specific workout."

"Oh yeah?" She flops back onto the bed. "Then I'm all yours, partner. Tell me what you need."

I'm not sure how long we spend in that bed, but she really

seems to enjoy having me tell her how and where and when to move, my instructions clarified with guidance from my hands, my words punctuated with kisses.

Maybe it's that she needs a break from being the one in charge, but I really don't care who's the captain of the ship, I just love taking my time with this woman. Eliciting every kind of sigh and groan you could imagine, watching her skin flush and shudder, her muscles tense and release. By the time I'm on my side spooning her so I can thrust from behind, it takes everything I've got to keep things slow.

That's when she takes the wheel, reaching between her legs to circle until inner walls pulse around my cock. When she arches her back and cries out, I'm done. I was kidding about the PT, but my hip flexors get a workout like none other as I piston into her. I can tell I've hit the spot when she stops moving and begins keening in a way that makes me wild. Gripping her hips, thumbs screwing into her ass cheeks, I let go, and she breaks all over again. Waves of pleasure coursing between us, I don't know where she ends and I begin.

Eventually, our breathing gets back to normal. But I don't think anything else about my world will be normal ever again. My boss just cracked it right open.

## HELEN

Despite the fact that we don't fall asleep until late, I wake up at three o'clock in the morning. Like I usually do. It's always a crapshoot whether I'll get back to sleep, but tonight, with no bookkeeping to go over in my head, my odds don't look good.

I do have to pee, so I get up and find my way to the bathroom without turning on the lights, walking a little bowlegged as I do. It's been a while since my last sexual escapade, but even then, I don't think I've ever had sex three times in one day. When I'm done, I tiptoe to the kitchen to get some water.

As I creep back toward the bed, Sully begins to thrash under the covers. A strangled moan sounds from behind closed lips, so full of pain it echoes in my heart. Not sure if I should wake him—I always forget whether it's sleepwalking or nightmares you're not supposed to disrupt, if either—I get close enough to stop him if it looks like he's in danger of hurting himself.

Just when it gets to the point that I can't stand watching him anymore, he sits up abruptly, gasping for air.

"Sully," I whisper.

He turns to face me, eyes wide.

"It's okay. You were dreaming."

"I—I… I was dreaming," he repeats.

Crawling onto the bed, I lay a hand on his forearm and give it a gentle squeeze. He shakes his head and shudders, like a dog shaking water off its coat. Gradually, his breathing slows, and he clears his throat.

I give him the glass of water I just filled before sliding under the covers next to him.

"Do you… want to tell me about it?"

He doesn't say anything for several long moments, so I add, "Or we could just try and go back to sleep."

He pinches the bridge of his nose. "I'm sorry I woke you."

"You didn't. I was up"—I twirl a hand in the direction of the bathroom—"taking care of business."

His hand drops, and he turns to me, blinking with obvious confusion. "You were working?"

I give him a playful slap. "No, dummy, it's a euphemism. I was peeing."

He rubs his face, laughing hollowly. "Ugh. Not really here."

After taking the water glass and setting it back on the nightstand, I lie down on my side facing him.

His focus is elsewhere, his eyes staring into space. Just as my own start to flutter closed, he says, "You don't seem like a pet kind of person."

I'm pretty sure I didn't fall asleep and miss half of a conversation, but I can't say for sure, so I ignore what seems like a total non sequitur. "Um… I haven't been for a long time. My schedule's too crazy. But I had a cat growing up and… she was important to me."

I won't share how my dad used to threaten to poison the cat, or dropkick the cat out the back door, or wring its neck. Not for anything the cat did. It was just another way to get at me and my mom. Sully needs the space to feel whatever he's dealing, not get mired in my unhappy childhood.

"Mr. Jones was important to me too," he says, his voice rough. "He seemed to know when I was down, would be more cuddly than usual. I shouldn't have taken him on the trip, but I was selfish. I didn't want to be lonely."

"How long did you have him?"

"Since senior year of college. I found him behind a fast-food place near the apartment building I was living in. He was a tiny thing but already scrappy. Too young to be away from his mama. I had to bottle-feed him for a while."

The image of this tall, broad-shouldered man cradling a tiny kitten melts even my jaded heart and has me reaching out to touch him. He pulls my hand to his chest as he continues.

"He could be a little jerk—like you'd be in the middle of petting him, and he'd get this look in his eye and bite you—but I loved him. When I moved to LA, I didn't take him at first. I'd only planned to drive across the country with Ford, but then I got a job, and then another one. I was there about a year before I went home and flew him back with me."

"Where was he all that time?"

"Violet, Dani, and Whitney lived together, and they kept him." He turns to face me, tucking my hand with his under his chin like we're sharing secrets at a sleepover. At least what I imagine a sleepover would be like since I never had one. "Violet claims he was always a community cat, but that's bullshit. He only loved me."

"Oh, yeah? He professed his love for you?"

He nods solemnly. "In his way, he did."

"How long were you in LA?"

"About seven years," he says over a yawn. "But it felt like seventeen."

"Why did you stay if you didn't like it?"

"At first, I needed the time to fix things with Ford. Then the work kept coming, and it felt stupid to say no."

"Right. You started telling me about that fight on the way up here. And then we missed the exit." When he doesn't say anything further, I ask, "What happened with you and Whitney and Ford?"

A grimace tilts the classic lines of his face. "You really want to hear about that?"

I'm not sure I do, but curiosity wins, even as *like, the thing that killed the cat?* echoes in my head. "Why not?"

He rolls onto his back before continuing. "Ford and I fought over Whitney. Twice. Before we moved to LA and then again just a couple months ago."

His head rocks back and forth, and his attention shifts to some movie in his head. " When we came back to Wallington with a movie last spring, after all those years away, I thought we were over her. But it just started right back up again. Same with my family. Like any growing up I'd done while I was away just flew out the window the minute I got home."

He glances over at me. "Does that happen when you go home? To New York?"

"Not really." What I don't say is: *I wouldn't know because I haven't gone back.* I walked out of the house I grew up in the day my mother died and haven't seen it or my father since.

He turns to face the ceiling again. "Whatever the reason, Ford and me fell right back into the 'who does Whitney love more' contest until—" He blows out a breath. "Until I asked her to go away with me on the boat this summer and she—"

"Wait. You asked her to go with you?" I blurt, my heart now wide awake and pulsing with something that feels an awful lot like jealousy.

He frowns. "Not just asked. I gave her an ultimatum."

"And she said no."

"She not only said no, she went and married a guy we all hated growing up, her most of all."

I'm doing my best to push away the green-eyed monster, but he must sense the tension, because he presses my hand to his chest. "Once I was out on the boat, by myself and away from everyone, it didn't take long for me to figure out that it really had nothing to do with being in love with her. It was more about winning. Like, if I won her—in this crazy lifelong competition with Ford—I'd feel better. About myself. But she never chose either of us. And... this is probably weird, but through all that drama, Mr. Jones was the only thing that kept me sane."

Still holding my hand, he drapes his other arm over his face. "And then I got him killed."

After a beat, I ask, "Are you really sure he's gone?"

"My parents put up signs near the accident when I was in the hospital. Nobody ever called." His free hand flails at the ceiling. "I mean, maybe he swam to shore, and someone found him. I hope that's the case. I just wish I knew."

"Is that… is that what you were dreaming about?"

"Actually…" He turns to face me again and traces a finger down my hairline, to the side of my jaw to my neck. "I don't remember anymore."

"Well, that's good."

"You're a good listener. Thank you."

"Anytime."

After giving me a sweet kiss, he tucks my hand back into his chest. "Goodnight, O'Neill."

"Goodnight, Calloway."

# CHAPTER 18

"How often we feel like loving someone but we are unable to do it."

–*Life is Beautiful*

## SULLY

OVER THE NEXT TWO DAYS, we split our time between bed, water, and table.

I still can't swim, but our cabin has a hot tub and the resort has paddle boats we take out on the river, which turns out to be excellent physical therapy. In addition to the workout my hip flexors and glutes get with Helen, that is.

Since it's Crab Fest, we join hundreds of other visitors for the big feast, where picnic tables covered with butcher paper are set up under tents. For just twenty bucks they give you nutcrackers and a bib and a bucket full of locally caught blue crab. Helen's never picked crab before, but by the end of the night, she's extracting every bit of the good stuff from the Old Bay seasoning-encrusted shells.

Watching her lick her fingers has me planning to cook up all kinds of seafood for her back in Wallington.

If she'll let me, that is.

I tell myself that I'm simply enjoying this time with her moment by moment, but if I'm honest, I'm just too chicken-shit to ask what's going to happen when we go back to North Carolina. As the clock ticks down, however, the question buzzes around in my head like a swarm of no-see-ums. Our last night, while we're relaxing in the cabin's hot tub, I go over all the possibilities in my head.

One, we just go back to how things were and pretend this never happened.

The wrong-answer buzzer sounds in my head.

Two, we could date when we get back to Wallington. I have nothing against taking her out, but since we spend so much time working, typical dates would be tough. Most restaurants don't welcome people waltzing in for dinner at 9:00 p.m. on a weekday.

Therefore, what's behind door number two gets the wrong-answer buzzer as well.

Three, we could keep doing what we've been doing this weekend in the bits of free time we have. This seems reasonable to me, but I have a feeling Helen will have reservations, just because she's my boss.

Which leads me to option number four.

"Do I need to quit for this to keep going?"

"Huh?" Helen opens one eye and squints at me from the other side of the tub.

I've been lazily massaging her feet in my lap as I think, and now I give them both a squeeze and release them to sit up straight. "I'm not ready for this to be over, and I want to do whatever will make it work, even if it means I have to find another job..."

My words trail away as she flaps at the steam billowing between us. When she doesn't say anything, I force out a more difficult question. "Unless... you don't want to keep doing this?"

She opens her mouth and closes it a few times before sliding deeper into the water with a groan. "If we could stay in this bubble, it'd be one thing." After dragging fingernails through her hair, making a few pieces stand on end, she continues. "But I have to go back to work."

"*You* have to go back to work? So you agree? That I should quit?"

"No, I don't want—" She rests the back of her head on the edge of the tub and looks up at the sky. "I *can't* lose you at the office and I do have to go back, like, tomorrow."

"I was planning on that too. Going back to Wallington, I mean. And then I'm laid off for another week, right?"

"Right." She sighs, eyes still on the sky. "Sorry about that."

"It's fine. I can use the time to hit the physical therapy hard, and deal with the insurance company."

"And a lawyer?"

"Ugh. We'll see."

Her head lolls to the side and she catches my eye. "Sully, will you please just talk to the guy I found? We could stop in Richmond on the way back."

"Why are you so set on me getting a lawyer?"

"Why are you so against it?"

The true, if-I'm-honest-with-myself reason? *Because my dad wants me to get one.* But that makes me sound like a fourteen-year-old, so instead I snap back, "Why are you so against us working together and being together?"

"It looks bad for me to be dating my assistant."

"Men do it all the time."

She sits up, spine stiff. "You have no idea what it's like to be a woman in this industry."

"You're right, I don't. So explain it to me."

"There's no way you'd understand."

"I'd like the chance to try," I say quietly.

She runs a wet hand through her hair, scrubbing at her scalp, her focus now on the woods surrounding us. "No matter how good I am, how long my list of credits is, I have to prove myself all over again every single time I take a job."

"But what does that have to do with—"

"If I show any vulnerability, any softness," she cuts in, her tone and expression stony, "then any authority I worked so hard to establish is *gone*. Kaput. I may as well quit because my ability to make the tough calls has been erased. I can't tell the cinematographer that we aren't going to break the bank to pay for some fancy lens that he just wants because it's the latest toy when he knows I've got a boy toy waiting for me back at the office."

"Is that what you think of me?"

She blows out a breath. "Of course not, but other people will. I'm a decade older than you, you're a hot young thing, and I'm your boss."

"If that is truly the only barrier, then I quit."

She sits up even taller and crosses her arms. "You can't file for unemployment if you quit."

I roll my eyes. "Then fire me."

She shakes her head, her lips pursed. "Mm-mm."

"No? You refuse to fire me?"

She nods her head. "You're too good."

Narrowing my eyes at her, I move ever so slowly through the water. Her brows rise, but she doesn't move, even as my hands come to rest on either side of her hips. Nuzzling her neck, teasing her with kisses and nips, I keep up my assault until she's squirming. "I'm good in other places too."

She groans. "You are, dammit."

"Let's be good together. At the office and in your bed."

"But—"

I cover her mouth with mine to stop her excuses.

After a long, lingering kiss, I whisper, "Give us a chance, O'Neill. I'll make it worth your while."

## HELEN

Sully's exceptionally persuasive. Even with an only partly healed broken leg, he's managed to make my body feel things I've never before experienced in places I didn't know existed, making my lengthening-by-the-day to-do list flutter to the back of my mind.

But the fact that I'm now sleeping with my assistant won't be ignored. My very first job in the industry—as someone's assistant—ended in a way that still haunts me, no matter how many times I shove it all back where it belongs: in my rearview mirror.

As I pack my bag Monday morning and do an idiot check of the cabin, a part of me wants to stay in this idyll forever, but I just can't stop thinking that I'm supposed to be working.

Probably because there's work to do. A pause in production won't stop the messages from piling up. Despite all the groundwork laid last week, Glenda will be in the office rescheduling locations and extending housing leases and attending to myriad other details cropping up. I should be there to help.

Sully has a meeting with the insurance adjuster back at the police boat yard before we leave town, and I'm hoping that'll give him the nudge he needs to contact a lawyer. It's probably good he'll have a chance to do his own idiot check there before they haul the boat off to fix it up, too.

We're both quiet as we straighten up the cabin. After we load our bags into the back of my rental, however, Sully leans his cane against the rear of the car and opens his arms wide.

I now know what the gesture means. He wants a hug. I've never known a man who hugs like Sully Calloway. He wants them often, and he does them well. Strong arms encircle me, making me feel precious. As I rest my cheek against his upper chest and tuck my head under his chin, his calm invites the little tensions that've built up in my mind and body over the past few hours to dissipate. We just breathe together, and for the first time, he ends the hug before I do.

# CHAPTER 19

"Don't let anyone ever make you feel like you don't deserve what you want."

*–10 Things I Hate About You*

## SULLY

IT'S EASIER FACING *Endless Summer* today than it was Friday. I'm more prepared, and I'm actually eager to hear what the adjuster has to say. It's still difficult to imagine that I'll be able to take her out again, but after the insurance guy goes over his paperwork with me and explains the repairs they will and will not cover, I'm cautiously optimistic. If all goes well, we'll both be seaworthy at around the same time—late spring of 1999.

After I sign the paperwork and shake hands with the adjuster, I head back to the main office, where Helen's using the pay phone to make calls before we drive back. When I step inside the main building and scan the offices, it's not Helen that catches my eye, however.

It's a little black cat.

*What the fuck?*

"Mr. Jones?"

## HELEN

I catch Sully's entrance out of the corner of my eye, and finish jotting down a few notes as Glenda fills me in on what's cropped up this morning. Before I can ask her if she's heard from the LA office, however, an odd yowling sound penetrates the glass of the phone nook's closed doors. When I locate the source of the sound, all I can see through the scratched glass is that Sully's got some black thing on his shoulder. A black thing that moves.

Assuring Glenda that I'll be back in the office later today, I hang up and pull the handle of the old door, which squeaks as it slides open.

Sully turns at the sound, the biggest grin I've ever seen lighting up his face. The thing making the noise and lounging on his shoulders is a small black cat.

"It's Mr. Jones!" he says, his voice full of wonder.

"Mr. Jones your cat?"

"Yeah, he… he's been here all this time."

Darla seems as shocked as he, as does the officer who steps into the front room.

"That's *your* cat?" the man asks.

"Yeah," Sully says, his eyes bright.

It seems as though he's too overwhelmed to speak, so I jump in. "His cat was on the boat when the accident happened."

"Oh, my word," Darla says, lengthening her vowels impressively. "He must've still been inside when they towed it here."

"Blackie did show up right around the time that sailboat did," the officer adds, hitching up his belt.

The receptionist reaches out to the cat, and it rubs its face against her hand. "Poor little Blackie."

Sully must've dropped his cane to pick up the cat, and he looks a little wobbly. I hand it to him, but it seems to be a struggle to juggle it and Mr. Jones. "I can't believe he's been here all this time."

"Well, he didn't have a tag with your number or anything, did he?" Darla's tone is full of reprimand.

Sully looks sheepish as he admits, "He doesn't like collars. Always managed to get 'em off."

"I tried to give him a proper name." The receptionist rolls her eyes. "But the guys just kept calling him Blackie."

"Good thing you saw him today," another officer says.

Seems the entire crew has moved into the reception area, as another guy chimes in with, "Yeah, somebody narced on us, and the head office was gonna make us take him to the SPCA."

"Even though he's kept the mouse population down."

"He is a good little hunter," Sully says proudly.

When it seems like they could go on like this forever, I interrupt. "I'm so sorry, but we've got to get on the road."

"Oh, jeez. I'm sorry, Helen," Sully says, turning his attention to me. "Um, are you okay with Mr. Jones riding back with us?"

"Of course," I say, wondering how that's going to work, since we don't have a carrier or anything. "As long as he's okay with it."

## SULLY

He isn't exactly "okay with it." The moment the engine starts, Mr. Jones scrambles out of my arms, crawls under my seat, and starts to make a god-awful moaning sound.

"So, is he named after that Counting Crows song?" Helen has to raise her voice to be heard over the din. "He kind of sounds like the lead singer."

"Nah, I got him before that came out. The name just came to me. But he does like their music." I put a CD mix in, hoping that it'll either soothe him or drown him out.

When it doesn't, Helen asks, "Is he okay?"

"Yeah, he'll settle down. Right, buddy? Life is good!" My boat's going to get repaired, Mr. Jones is alive, my leg's getting stronger every day, and I've somehow managed to seduce the hottest and smartest woman I've ever met.

Now all I have to do is convince her that it's a good idea to keep this thing going. Once the cat quiets, I begin formulating my strategy by assessing what I know about her.

On food: she loved the meals we had this weekend, but she doesn't like to cook.

My plan: wow her with meals cooked with local ingredients.

On music: her tastes are as eclectic as mine.

My plan: make her a mix CD of my favs, from Counting Crows and Shawn Colvin to the head-banging rock we listened to on the way up.

To continue my research, I ask about her movie preferences and learn that we agree on horror movies like *Se7en* and *Silence of the Lambs*—saw 'em but kind of wish we hadn't (wack nightmares). Same for *Scream* and *I Know What You Did Last Summer* but for different reasons (waste of time).

Weirdly, I've seen more rom-coms than she has.

"Why is that?" she asks.

"Because I get dragged to them by Violet."

Mostly we both like movies that take risks. Oscar winners like *Life is Beautiful*, but also smaller movies like *Pump Up the Volume*.

"I worked on that director's second movie," Helen says.

"*Empire Records*? That was shot in Wallington."

"Right. That's when I met Dani," she says.

"On the subject of Wallington," I begin, since we've made it to I-40 and are within spitting distance of home, "are you really going to pretend you don't want to have sex with me when we get back?"

"Sully," she says. "That's not it at all."

"Good. Then we can keep hanging out and having lots of excellent sex?"

"You're not listening to me."

"I'm sorry." I turn in my seat so I'm facing her. "I am all ears and ready to hear any sensible reason why you want to end something that was pretty awesome all weekend."

She shoots a look over at me but quickly returns her eyes to the road. "In addition to all the issues I brought up last night, I don't want people to resent you and think that you're getting special treatment because you're having an affair with me."

I don't like the word "affair," which feels like it's minimizing what I already feel for her, but I wait this time to make sure she's finished. "Okay. That makes sense. So, what if we keep our relationship the same as it's been at work, but when we're not at work, we… see where things go?"

She opens her mouth like she's going to argue, then closes it. I can almost see her having an argument in her head so I bide my time, hoping that my side wins. Eventually she bites her lip and looks over at me.

I give her a hopeful grin.

"It has to stay a secret," she says, speaking slowly and emphasizing each word.

I nod decisively. "If that's what you need, then that's what you get. The existence of mind-blowing sex and other good times between Helen O'Neill and Sullivan Calloway will remain just between us."

She glances over one more time.

"Until you decide otherwise." Just as I add the final word, two little paws stretch between my feet, and Mr. Jones emits a pitiful mew. "Look who woke up."

I pick him up and settle him on my lap. "Ready to see your archenemy again, little buddy?"

## HELEN

After I drop Sully and his belongings at Dani's house, I head straight to the office, needing to be in a place where I can at least pretend to be in control. Even when faced with the kind of shitshow I've been handed with this project.

Like all of the below-the-line staff, I'm paid on a weekly basis and am technically laid off. But the above-the-line folks —the people who are either paid a flat fee or who have a stake in the movie—won't stop asking questions. There's no way I'm waiting until next week to deal with it all, especially since I know Glenda's doing the same.

After I go through phone messages and emails that have built up since I left Friday, I head over to the production coordinator's office. The door's ajar, but the lights are off and the place seems empty.

"Hello? Anybody home?"

I find Glenda backlit by the late afternoon light streaming through a window. We spend a few minutes divvying up calls to make and fires to put out. Then she sits back in her desk chair and tips her head to the side as she studies me. "Huh. You got laid this weekend."

"What? I did no—I mean, I—"

"Oooh, you did. Who was it?" She sits up straight. "Oh my god, did you finally bed your hunk of an assistant?"

"What? How can you tell?" I scrub both hands over my face. "Dammit. It's supposed to be a secret."

"Why would you keep him a secret?" Glenda grins and slaps her desk. "Spill, woman. I need some good news."

# CHAPTER 20

"If I succeed in loving you, I will be able to love everyone and all species on Earth... This is the real message of love."

—Thich Nhat Hanh, *Teachings on Love*

## SULLY

HELEN SWIMS NEXT TO ME, her limbs sweeping through the water. Suddenly, she turns, feet pushing off of my chest as she kicks away. When she bursts through the water's surface, she makes the weirdest sound.

Gasping, blinking my eyes open, it takes a moment to register that I'm not in the water. Instead, I'm on a couch in the middle of a fight between a barking dog and a hissing cat.

"Is that Mr. Jones?" Dani asks from the doorway.

"Mr. Jones?" Violet echoes from her side.

With a "mrrrow" the cat in question takes off with Skye in hot pursuit.

"Shit," I mutter as I push to standing.

"The dog door's open!" Dani yells.

"I'll get it!" Violet sprints for the back door while Dani and I follow the cat and dog down the hall.

I round the corner in time to see Dani disappear into her bedroom, followed by a loud crash. I get there just in time for Mr. Jones to bank off my groin with a screech, followed by Skye who knocks me into the doorframe on her way out.

"Goodness gracious, are you okay?" Dani asks.

"Ugh. I'll survive." Straightening with a groan, I catch sight of the broken lamp on her bedroom floor. "Doing better than your lamp, anyway."" I wince at the sight of the broken lamp lying across her bedroom floor.

"Damn cat," she mutters.

"The dog started it," I protest.

"Whatever. Let's try and catch 'em before they do more damage."

After what seems like an hour but is probably only a few minutes, the three of us manage to get ahold of Skye. With the cat hissing underneath my bed, we drag her out of the room and shut the door, trapping Mr. Jones inside. Then Dani puts the dog in the backyard, and we all collapse on the couch.

"Welcome back," Dani croaks.

"Thanks."

"So what the fuck? How did you find him?" Violet asks.

As I answer questions about what happened over the weekend, I swear I never breathe a word about Helen. But once their curiosity is satisfied regarding the cat and the boat, the two women go through some silent communication before crossing their arms in unison and then putting me back in the spotlight for a long moment.

"What?" I finally ask.

Dani smiles sweetly. "Since you're hooking up with Helen now, can you ask her to keep the cat?"

## HELEN

The man could sell me sand in a desert and convince me that I got a bargain. One phone call, and I'm now Mr. Jones's landlady. One grin, and all the reasons why I needed to get work done this evening disappear from my head. One kiss, and I'm ripping both our clothes off and dragging him into the bedroom.

However, after our post-dinner round of sex—not to be confused with the pre-dinner round, which we went at like we hadn't made love before leaving the cabin in Virginia just this morning—the worries start up.

If Glenda figured out that Sully and I are sleeping together, if we can't keep our hands off each other, it won't be long before everyone's staring at the two of us, wondering what's going on, wondering what that means for my professionalism, wondering what he's getting out of this—

Sully takes my hand, which I'd apparently been dragging through my hair, and gives my knuckles a kiss. "Hey, um, I should've said something earlier, but I need to tell you something."

My eyes pop open to find a pained expression on his face. "Did we just hurt your leg?"

He coughs out a low laugh. "No, uh… I mean, there was a tricky moment when I had you bent over the back of the couch. Almost lost my balance. But no. My leg's fine."

He pauses and I almost tell him to spit it out, when I realize I should tell him that Glenda knows about us. "Actually, I have something to—"

"I should go first. Not to be ungentlemanly, but you might be mad and not want to tell me yours."

This has me sitting up. "Okay."

"Dani and Violet know about us."

"You told them?"

"No, of course not. But Dani somehow guessed, and Violet

was right there. I couldn't lie to them, and it'd be useless anyway."

"Yeah." I flop onto my back again. "Glenda guessed too."

His eyes widen. "No way."

"Way." Rolling my head back and forth against the arm of the couch, I let out an exasperated breath. "I guess we have to go into damage control."

"Oh" is all he has to say in response.

When I open my eyes again, the expression on his face is so bereft, I crawl over to sit on his lap. "Sully, I'm not mad, but if the word's going to get out, I want to be the one to tell our colleagues, rather than have people talking about me behind my back. I hate that feeling."

"I gotcha." Then he brightens. "But hey. We have another week till everyone is back."

Running my nails down his spine, I circle my hips. "Guess we should make the most of it."

He squeezes my butt cheeks, which fit perfectly in his palms. "Women really do hit their sexual peak in their thirties, huh?"

"Pfft. It's not like you're having trouble keeping up with me."

"It's not easy. But I survived a boat wreck. I think I can handle you. And if I'm wrong, can't think of a better way to go."

"Oh, uh... not to get sidetracked or anything, but speaking of surviving a boat wreck. Does the cat need any, you know, supplies?"

"I fed him his dinner and put out his bowls then. Didn't you see?"

"No, I mean, like a litter box."

"Oh. Gotcha." He nods. "Glad you brought that up. We need to show him the toilet, and you'll have to keep the toilet seat up."

"Why?" I laugh. "Is he going to use it?"

"Yep."

"The cat uses the toilet," I repeat, not sure we're on the same page. "Not just goes in the bathroom somewhere. He squats on the actual toilet."

"He pees and poops right in the bowl." Sully holds up a hand. "He does not flush, however."

"How in the hell did you make that happen?"

"It wasn't me. The girls befriended this animal trainer when I was in LA, and Lucy helped them train him. I guess it took some patience, but he's used it ever since. Even on the boat."

"Why can't this same trainer get the dog to stop chasing the cat?"

"It wasn't a big deal before because they never had to live together. The cat and I were in LA or living on the boat, and the girls just adopted Skye this past year. They wanted her to be a communal dog, but—" He breaks off with a shudder. "One night of the dog and the cat on the boat made it clear that wasn't going to be so easy. But now that I might be staying with Dani for a while, we'll get on that. Don't worry, you don't need to keep him forever."

"Well, good. Because I won't be here forever."

Lips pressed together, he just nods. Because I'm a coward, I change the subject. "Before you make me lose my mind again, let's show him the toilet. Whatever that means."

After I wrap myself in Sully's flannel shirt and he pulls his boxers on, Sully finds Mr. Jones, carries him to the bathroom, and sets him on the toilet seat. Then he backs out and leaves the door slightly ajar. Apparently, the little guy likes his privacy. A few minutes later, Mr. Jones stalks back into the living room, tail high. Sully gestures, and we creep back to the toilet, where there's a little cloud of yellow.

"Wow," I say. "That's a game changer."

After Sully presses the lever, I ask, "The cat can't flush?"

"I guess you can teach them to, but apparently some cats

get fascinated with the swirling water and end up flushing over and over again. That adds up on your water bill."

"I bet it does."

Sully draws me in for a hug. "Thanks for letting him stay here. I know it's a lot to ask."

"If you can teach him to make coffee, he can stay as long as he wants."

Leaning back, Sully raises an eyebrow. "I can make coffee. And bring it to you in bed."

"Wait a minute. I thought you"—I make air quotes—"couldn't bring me coffee."

"I couldn't," he admits. "But now that I'm only on the cane, I can. And, if my appointment tomorrow goes well, I might even be cane-free."

"I'd like to see this new ability of yours, so I suppose you'll have to stay the night."

Backing me toward the bedroom, he says, "Oh, I've got all sorts of abilities you haven't seen yet, missy."

And then he proceeds to show them to me, one by one.

# CHAPTER 21

> "To take good care of ourselves, we must go back and take care of the wounded child inside of us."
>
> —Thich Nhat Hanh

## SULLY

WHEN I LEAVE the doctor's office the next day, I'm high as a kite, and not on pain meds. My tibia is healing right on schedule, my strength and flexibility are where they need to be, and I've got the okay to lose the cane, which I've barely been using anyway.

I know I still have a long way to go before my balance will be good enough to even think about getting up on a board, and the doc doesn't want me doing anything that'd risk a fall, but I can finally see the light at the end of the tunnel.

Before I can escape the building, however, I'm supposed to talk to someone in the billing department. I know I need to sort everything out, but it still feels like being called into the principal's office. However, when I step inside, she doesn't yell at me. Instead, she asks if I want her to speak to my attorney.

"My attorney? Why?"

"Well, honey," she begins with bless-your-heart patience, "that's what a personal injury attorney does. He'll lien the file in favor of the medical provider who has rendered services, which means we know we'll get paid, and we stop bugging you. If he's good, you won't have to pay anything at all."

"Oh. Well, yeah. Can you give me the number he should call?"

She hands me the printout of my bill, which is literally an inch high. "Don't wait too long, honey. If we don't hear from y'all soon, it'll go to collections."

My mood having taken a deep dive into the crapper, I now need to decide whether to call this attorney or just pay this and the bills from the hospital in Virginia out of my savings. I've avoided calling the guy that Helen found, afraid that going through a lawsuit would keep me stuck in the past. Now, though, with Mr. Jones back from the dead, and the boat and my leg on the mend, there's a lot less anger and resentment in which to wallow.

Meaning, the only reason I haven't done it is because I'm stubborn and don't want to do something my dad wants me to.

As I walk toward the other end of the building where my car is parked, I remind myself of what I was feeling before I stepped into the billing office. While I do my best to replace the frustration with gratitude, something I heard in the tape I listened to on the way over comes back to me.

As Mr. Hanh would say, *Hello, Habit Energy.*

I'm beginning to understand that negative reactions to my father's suggestions are old habits, developed when I was a kid. The first step in unlearning a habit is to give it attention.

In doing so, I'm getting that just because I hear my parents' comments as judgmental, doesn't mean they are. Most likely, they want me to be happy, and are doing their best to protect me and guide me, but I've poisoned their words with my own jealousy and feelings of unworthiness.

According to the billing lady, hiring a lawyer in my situation is the sensible thing to do. I could just call the attorney Helen found, but I might kill two birds with one stone by asking my father for advice.

"Excuse me, do y'all have a pay phone?" I ask a receptionist near the building's front entrance.

"If it's a local call, you can use the one in there," she says, pointing to a vacant office across the hall.

"Thanks, it is."

My parents' teaching schedules change every semester, so I never know when they're home or at work, but my dad answers his office phone. The university's only ten minutes away, so he says to come on by.

"To what do I owe the pleasure?" he asks as he ushers me in. "Hey, no crutches?"

"Yeah, it just happened today. I still have a lot more physical therapy to do, but everything's on track."

"I guess we haven't seen you in a while," my dad says as he sits behind his desk. "Time flies at the beginning of the semester."

Noticing the flash of jealousy—the habitual but perhaps not accurate feeling that my parents care more about their work and students than they do about me—I set it aside and fill him in on my latest news, everything from finding Mr. Jones to the fact that the boat will likely be repaired. "But the whole thing with the insurance companies is more complicated than I thought. The medical billing person seemed to assume that I'd have an attorney to deal with it all."

I meet my father's gaze, and to his credit, he doesn't chime in with "I told you so." He just nods.

"I think it's time to take your suggestion and talk to a lawyer."

My dad tents his hands under his chin. "I've never had to

deal with that either, but a colleague of mine did when he was in a car accident."

"Helen—Ms. O'Neill, I mean—my boss at the moment, she found this guy, but he's up in Virginia."

As I dig the piece of paper with the guy's name out of my wallet, my dad says, "Well, that could be a positive, since the accident occurred in Virginia."

"Should I call him?"

"Can't hurt."

"Can I do it here so you can listen in? I'm just not sure what to say."

"Of course. Here." He takes the piece of paper. Dialing the number with one hand, he hands me a legal pad with the other. "For notes."

When a receptionist answers, my father explains that he and I were referred and that we'd like to ask a few questions. At first the woman says she'll take our names and numbers and call back, but then she says, "Oh, wait a moment, he just got off the line. I'll see if he can talk to you."

A moment later, a man's voice comes onto the line. "Murray Janus, who am I speaking with?"

My father gestures at me, so I introduce myself and explain that he's on speaker and my father is also present. Then I give him a quick rundown of the situation. After asking a few questions, he's silent for a few moments. Just when I'm about to ask if he's still on the line, he clears his throat.

"Look, I could go after this kid, net you a great deal of money, and ruin his life to boot. I'd have to do some research to be certain, but it sounds as though it'd be an open-and-shut case."

"And if I don't want to do that?"

"Do what? Get the money or punish the boat captain?"

"Neither." I shoot a quick glance at my father, but his

expression doesn't give his thoughts away. "I just want to make sure I can pay my bills."

"Then you don't want me. I'm a criminal lawyer. You need a decent personal injury lawyer."

"An ambulance chaser? That's what I wanted to avoid."

"Some are like that, not all. I can recommend someone reputable."

"And that would be better?"

"Kid, you can't afford me unless you're going for the jugular. Larry Lockwood, Jr. will make sure all your ducks are in a row. Me, I'd be shooting ducks out of the sky. You'll get a reasonable settlement for work hours lost and your medical bills will be covered."

"Okay, well, thanks for your time. I really appreciate it and the referral."

After he gives me the other lawyer's information, he says, "Tell Larry he owes me one," and hangs up.

My dad picks up the receiver and drops it back in the cradle to hang up on our end. I can't quite read his expression.

"Do you think I should've hired that guy?"

"It's not up to me," he says.

Not the answer I was hoping for. That is, a resounding no. "If I don't 'go for the jugular,' do you think the kid will learn the lesson and not do it again?"

He shrugs. "Hopefully, the higher insurance premium will be a deterrent. But you never know."

"I was a stupid teenager too," I say.

My dad just nods. "Most of us were."

I thank him again for his help, but before I make it to the door, he asks, "Hey, want to get some lunch?"

"Sure, Dad. That'd be good."

## HELEN

When Sully calls to tell me he has good news and he wants to celebrate, my first instinct is to maintain some sort of distance between us. "You sure you don't want to celebrate with your friends?"

"You'll appreciate one of these things more than they will. Plus, I owe you for taking the cat."

"You don't owe me any—"

"Woman, do you want a home-cooked meal or not?"

"I have no idea if my kitchen even has pots and pans," I warn him. "And I'm not ready to get all domestic at your roommate's house."

"I checked your kitchen out when I made coffee this morning. The knives and sauté pan are useless, but I can bring my cooking stuff from the boat to supplement." Before I can come up with another excuse, he asks, "When do you want to eat?"

I tell him I have a call with the LA people in an hour, and he asks if he can come by and pick up a key to my place so he can have dinner ready when I'm done. It seems like both a terrible idea and a wonderful idea. Who wouldn't want to come home to a handsome man cooking her dinner? But at the same time, a girl could get used to it and then be devastated when the show's over.

But because I can't say no to Sully, he gets his way.

When I walk into my apartment, the scent of garlic has my mouth watering and my stomach telling me I forgot to eat lunch.

When I step into his embrace, strong arms ease the tension I acquired over the course of the day. After he releases me, he pours me a glass of wine. "Take a load off. Dinner will be ready shortly."

Instead of sitting, I follow my nose to the stove. "What are you making?"

"Shrimp scampi and a salad. Simple stuff." He shoos me away. "Sit your ass down. This kitchen ain't big enough for the two of us."

I do as he asks, taking a sip of the crisp white as he moves with grace and efficiency from the stove to the sink to the counter. From chopping parsley, to tossing shrimp in a pan, to the addition of what looks like a homemade stock, he definitely looks like he knows what he's doing.

And then it hits me. "You're not using your cane!"

He shoots a grin over his shoulder. "I was wondering when you were going to notice."

"Sorry, I was distracted by your Julia Child imitation. Is that one of the pieces of good news?"

"It is. Doc says I'm healing right on schedule. Can't surf until the bone's more solidly healed, and I need to stay on top of the therapy, but I'm going to be walking without a hitch very soon. I'll be mostly back to normal by the first of the year."

*Which means he can go back to working in the sound department.*

Tabling that thought, I jump up and help him carry the plates to the table he's already set. "What's the other news?"

"I got a lawyer."

"Wow. What changed your mind?"

"It became clear that I need someone to sort out all the insurance crap and the bills. I talked to the guy you found, but we agreed he wasn't the best choice. He referred me to someone else."

"So long as you're covered."

"My dad helped me sort through it, and I think I am now, yeah." He lifts his wine glass. "To you. Without your help, things wouldn't be working out as well as they have."

My cheeks warm as I clink my glass to his. "I don't know about that, but I'm happy for you."

When I dig into the pasta—angel hair loaded with

garlicky shrimp—I can't help but moan. "Oh my god, this is awesome."

"Well, it starts with the ingredients. Carolina shrimp is the best, and this was caught this morning."

"How do you know?"

"Guy at Eagle Island seafood told me. I always get whatever's freshest and build the meal around it."

"Who taught you to cook like this?"

"I worked in a hotel kitchen on and off during college, but really it was my parents. They're both academics, so they were able to arrange their schedules so one or the other would always be home to make dinner, but both me and my brother had to help."

As we eat, I learn more about his family. Even though he complains that his older brother is the favored son, it's clear they're all close. Like they're the Keatons or the Cleavers, while my parents and me... we're more like the Bunkers or the Bundys. Without the laugh track.

When he offers me a second helping, I lean back and rub my full belly. "It was amazing, but I couldn't eat another bite. You're going to make me fat as it is."

"Fine with me," he says.

"Guess I'll have to work it off later," I say, with a waggle of my eyebrows in case he misses my point.

"Also fine with me," he says, his waggle matching mine.

# CHAPTER 22

"You'll know when you meet the right girl because it's not how you feel about her, it's how she makes you feel about yourself."

—*The Wedding Singer*

## SULLY

I GOTTA SAY, I'm loving my schedule right now. If only I could surf, it'd be perfect. But the past week has been pretty damn awesome even without plying my board on the waves.

I wake with a gorgeous woman by my side and my resurrected cat warming my feet. When I bring the former coffee in bed, her grateful smile lights up the room. If I get her up early enough, we can even fit in a little horizontal boogie before she has to go to work.

When she leaves, I clean up the kitchen and straighten up around the apartment—sometimes putting in a load of laundry—before heading either to my home gym or to work with Ronnie at her therapy clinic. I meet a friend or parent for lunch and then go to the market, do an errand or two, then check in with Helen so I can have dinner ready when she gets home. We eat a healthy, delicious meal and then go for a walk or watch a movie or read in bed together. Sometimes she sneaks work in too, but I can always distract her.

If a genie said I could live like this forever, I'd take it. Reality's looking a little different. *Hacked* starts up shooting again next week and then it wraps the first week of December. When I called my union's insurance company, I found out that while I got an extension on my benefits because of the accident, it ends as soon as I'm cleared to return to work.

Which means I need a sound department job that starts up early in 1999.

So today, after my workout, I head over to the studio. Not to see Helen, but to do a little schmoozing, hoping to gather intel on productions coming into town. Neither Vi nor Nate nor Dani have news for me, but I do find Ford on a *Lawson's Reach* set. He introduces me to the sound mixer, who's from Los Angeles.

While Ford watches rehearsal, I chat with the guy. Turns out he knows all of the mixers we worked with out in California.

"It's a small community," he acknowledges. "Did you grow up here too?"

"Yup, but we moved out to LA right after college. Worked out there for seven years, but I'm hoping to find more work here in town going forward."

"And you're on *Hacked* right now? Or you were?" When I nod, he whistles. "I've heard a lot of crazy stories, but I never heard of a show shutting down for an appendix."

"Me neither. I'm not the cable guy on *Hacked,* though. I broke my leg a couple months ago, and I took an office job while it's healing."

He looks me up and down. "Looks like both legs are working fine now."

"Getting there," I explain. "But I'm still a little wobbly."

"You must be going crazy working in the office."

I shrug. "I don't hate it, but I do miss being on set. And I need an IATSE job to get my insurance hours."

"Gotcha. Well, I'll tell Ford if I hear about anything."

When they break for lunch, Ford and I find a table together. "Thanks for the introduction to your mixer, man. He seems cool."

He nods and starts shoveling food into his mouth, but then pauses to send me a smirk. "I heard you've got a sugar mama."

I stop with a forkful of chicken halfway to my mouth. "Huh?"

"A hot older woman?" He looks around before leaning closer. "Your boss?"

"Dammit. Those girls are the biggest gossips."

He starts eating again, talking with his mouth full. "Didn't hear it from them. Heard it from this girl I'm dating, who is roommates with a girl who's a PA in the production coordinator's office."

"Man, Helen's gonna be pissed."

"She embarrassed to be with you? I mean, I can see why."

I know he's just giving me shit, but my feelings on the subject must be obvious, because he reaches over the table to punch me on the arm. "I'm just kidding, man."

"I know," I say with a sigh. "Touchy subject."

"Well, it'll be over soon anyway. I mean, she's not hanging around after the show's over. And you're not going back to LA, are you?"

"I might have to if I can't find anything here. I need hours to keep my health insurance, or I'll be on the hook for my medical bills next year."

"That sucks."

Needing a change of subject, I circle back to the girl he mentioned. "New squeeze again this week? Dude, you're getting around."

He drops his gaze to his plate, shoving food around with his fork. "So? I'm young, I should be having fun."

I shift in the folding chair to stretch my leg. "We had some fun in California."

"We did," he says, his smile genuine. "Ford and Sully take LA."

"Remember that girl you dated who said she was an actress but turned out she was a princess at kids' parties?"

"She *was* an actress, you doof. That was her day job." His laughter fades as he stares off into space. "She was sweet."

"Funny how all those girls were petite blue-eyed blondes, but that girl who came to the beach a few weeks ago had dark hair."

"Yeah, well. I'm done with blondes." He sighs. "That wedding was surreal."

Because I've known him forever, and because I nudged him in this direction, I know whose wedding he's talking about.

"You went?"

He nods but doesn't look up. "Seemed like I should."

I was on the boat when it all went down, but even if I'd been in town, I don't know if I'd have been able to watch it.

"All those girls up there, perfectly put together, skinny as rails," Ford continues. "Whit looked like this fake version of herself. All hyped up and over the top."

"You think she was on drugs or something?"

"More like she was doing everything she could to convince herself she'd made the right choice. I only got to talk to her for a couple minutes, and she went on and on about the honeymoon in Bermuda they had planned. And the trousseau her mom bought her on a trip to Atlanta."

"What the hell is a trousseau?"

Ignoring my question, he adds, "But she wasn't really there. Like, it was Whitney's body and Whitney's voice, but somebody else had taken over her brain."

We just sit there in silence for a few minutes, but when Ford stands, saying something about needing to get back to work, I stop him.

"I need to say something, buddy." I wait until he meets my gaze to continue speaking. "I feel sorry for her. I think she's made a huge mistake, and I'm not sure why she did it. But I want you to know—what I thought I felt for her, I think it was really about you and me."

His butt drops back into his chair. "What are you talking about?"

"Even before I landed in the hospital, I had a lot of time to think. I love Whitney, the way I love all of you. But I only wanted her as a girlfriend because you did." I ball up my napkin and toss it onto my plate. "Fucked up, I know. But we've always had that competition thing between us."

"We have?"

He seems genuinely confused by my statement. "Yeah. I mean—from grades and sports to who could eat the most hot dogs."

"But, I mean, that wasn't serious. That was just—"

"Maybe it wasn't to you, but it was to me. Because in all the ways that counted, you always came out on top."

He looks off into the distance for a moment. "Except in the only competition I really cared about."

"Because neither of us got the girl?"

When he turns back to face me, his cheeks are flushed. "Honestly, I would've been jealous, but I sure as hell wish it'd been you who got her instead of that bastard."

## SULLY

Every Halloween, my friends and I stock up on candy and beer and burger fixings and play volleyball in Dani's front yard. The trick-or-treaters just add another level of challenge to the game. When they show up, play can't stop. A player from the team on the side closest to the front door has to run over and hand out the candy while his mates keep the ball in the air.

Since I'm injured this year, I'll referee. Right now, I'm grilling burgers while Nate and Ford hang lights out front so the game can continue until the kids go home. We've got a few other friends over too, including Ford's latest love interest. A different girl than the one he told me about just a few days ago.

"Where's Helen?" Dani asks after directing guests to the cooler for drinks.

I look meaningfully at the nearest guest. "Hush up, Dani. The whole world doesn't need to know about us. It's bad enough that you guys know."

"I think that cat's out of the bag," Violet says, plopping into a chair next to Dani. "Craft service Randy found out, so it'll be all over the lot before you know it."

"Ugh." I wince as I flip burgers. "It's gonna get awkward when we start back up Monday."

"What's the big dealio?" Dani hands me a beer. "It's not like people don't hook up on shows. It happens all the time."

"You don't do it," I point out.

"Yeah, but she's weird," Violet says.

"What's that supposed to mean?" Dani shoots back.

"I'm pretty sure the last time you went on a date, *My So-Called Life* was still on the air."

"On network TV, or when they showed the repeats on MTV?" I ask.

"Doesn't matter, it was still years ago," Vi says.

"That's not true. I went out with that guy on that show we did in—" Dani stops tossing the salad to think. "Oh. Yeah, okay. That was 1995."

"So, are you and Helen still together?" Vi asks.

Pretending that the burgers need my full attention, I shrug. "I mean, I don't know that we've ever been *together*. We hang out. I really like her, but I don't know how it could continue. I'm not moving back to LA unless I have no other choice."

"And she wouldn't relocate here? There's plenty of work. Nate's sister—she's the attorney in his dad's casting firm—claims it'll just keep coming. People love shooting here."

"Would you not want to keep seeing her?" Dani asks.

"Of course I would. She's awesome."

She points the salad tongs at me. "Did you invite her tonight?"

"I did, and she had some excuse for why she couldn't come."

"Maybe she hates kids," Violet says with a wince.

"I think she just wants to keep whatever we have going on the down-low."

Dani continues to gesture with the tongs. "She might not think you're serious and doesn't want to be embarrassed—"

"Or hurt," Vi adds.

"When you end it," Dani finishes.

Vi gasps. "But if we convinced her that Wallington is better than LA…"

"Then you'd have a better chance."

"Y'all've never even been to LA," I argue. When these girls get started there's no stopping them, but a man's got to try.

"I have," Violet says.

"For a couple days," I counter.

"And it was awful."

Nate appears out of nowhere to put his arm around Vi and direct a question to me. "Talking about my hometown?"

"No offense, man," I say. "But there're way the fuck too many people in LA. And cars. And the ocean's cold and polluted. But most of all, it's the seasons."

"Does it even have seasons? Isn't it seventy degrees, like, every day?" Dani asks.

"That's what people think, and it is like that a lot of the year—" Nate begins.

"But what's worse than lacking seasons," I cut in, "is when the season is just *wrong*. It freaked my body out big time."

"What are you talking about?" Vi asks.

"June Gloom and the Santa Anas in October." I shake my head as I begin to transfer burgers and dogs to a serving plate. "I'm not sure which was worse."

"I've never heard of either," Dani says, picking up the plate and holding it closer to the grill.

"Maybe it was just me, but when Memorial Day comes along and you're all ready for summer to start—"

"Oh, I love that feeling," Vi says on a sigh. "Time to get your toes in the sand."

"Well, forget that feeling in SoCal because in June, there's these low-hanging clouds, and it's like sixty degrees every day. Not cold, but not beach weather either."

"That does sound terrible," Violet says. "And what are Santa Anas?"

"Ugh. The Santa Anas are the worst," Ford says, coming out to the back patio from the kitchen. "You're all ready for sweater weather, for that nip in the air like we've got tonight, but these winds come in off the desert, and it's super dry and like ninety degrees for days on end."

"People get murderous," I say.

Nate nods. "Seriously, the crime rate goes up."

"I mean, we do have hurricanes here," Ford says. "And tourists."

"And they've got earthquakes," Violet argues. "While we've got the best spring in the world and just enough of a winter to make you want to get cozy inside."

"Doesn't sound like it'd be too hard to convince Ms. O'Neill to move away from that," Dani declares.

"Yep." Vi claps her hands. "We're on it."

"Guys. Don't get all—"

"Sully. Calm down. We got this." Vi checks her watch and then turns to the rest of crowd. "Time to eat, y'all. We are T-minus thirty for Trick-or-Treat Volleyball, so fuel up."

Dani sets the filled plate of cooked meat on the table before turning back to pat me on the shoulder. "Don't worry, dude. It'll be fine."

# CHAPTER 23

"It's Halloween; everyone's entitled to one good scare."

*—Halloween*

## HELEN

AM I jealous of Sully's *Family Ties* parents or his friends who hang out together as much as the ones at Central Perk?

God, yes.

Am I a big enough person to admit it?

Hell, no.

Therefore, when he very sweetly invites me to a party that somehow combines trick-or-treating with volleyball, I firmly decline, claiming to have my own plans.

Which I didn't, but that wasn't too difficult to change.

I may not have a single friend I've known since childhood —a time I'd rather forget—but I do have work friends. Principal photography starts back up Monday, so everyone's trickling back into town. It only takes a few calls before I've got a respectable number of women signed up for dinner and drinks Saturday night.

I told them this wasn't a Halloween thing, but I guess

when you're in the movie business, that request falls on deaf ears. Kara offered to be the designated driver, and I didn't argue after what happened the last time this crew went out. When she pulls up in front of my apartment building and the door of her SUV swings open to reveal costumed bodies, I almost turn tail and run.

"I told you she wouldn't dress up," Glenda says, fluffing the white sleeves of her low-cut dirndl, her long gray hair in braids wrapped on top of her head.

"Where're your sheep, Heidi?" I ask, my tone more caustic than I'd intended.

My question's ignored. Instead, Sherry hands me a shopping bag.

"What's this?"

"Your costume, silly. It's Halloween," Gemma says, patting me on the shoulder like she feels a bit sorry for me.

The makeup supervisor did go all out. Between the very convincing gashes on her face, a ghostly skin tone, and a dress hanging in tatters, it's pretty clear what she is. "Zombie?"

"*Sexy* zombie," she corrects.

I scan the other women's outfits. "Is that why everyone's wearing a corset? You're all 'sexy this' or 'sexy that'?"

"Not me," Nora says, adjusting her boobs, lifted by a corset that seems to be wrapped in gold. "I'm a Valkyrie. They're sexy by definition, so the descriptor would be redundant."

As Kara pulls onto Market Street and accelerates, I peer into the bag I was handed. "And what am I going to be?"

"Sexy boss, natch." Sherry shrugs. "Seemed obvious."

Thankfully, they don't make me don a corset. After we arrive at the Rumrunner—a beachfront hotel that's supposed to have a great dinner menu—the women escort me into the ladies' room to supervise my transformation. Sherry's costume for me includes a push-up bra, a deep-cut red silk blouse, a pin-striped business suit with a miniskirt, and red fuck-me pumps.

After I emerge from the stall in the getup, Gemma and Nora attack my face and hair. Moments later, I've got smoky eyes, red lips that match the blouse perfectly, and my hair is slicked straight back.

"You clean up good, girl," Glenda says with a wink.

"Hot, hot, hot," Gemma agrees, handing me the tube of lipstick. "You need to wear this shade all the time."

"All right, all right, calm down. We're going to be late for our reservation."

As our merry band troops into the dining room, I wonder why I don't make gatherings like this more of a priority. Once we've ordered and drinks arrive, however, I remember why.

Gossip.

At first everyone but me shares what they've been up to during the break, which includes Kara's announcement that she's pregnant with her first child.

"Wow, congratulations," I say, even as I think, *There goes your career, honey.*

But then, Nora gives me a speculative look. "So, tell us about your boy toy."

When I shoot a glare at Glenda, she goes hands up. "It wasn't me. The craft service guy found out and now…" She trails off.

"You're public knowledge," Sherry finishes.

"Girl, you're just lucky it wasn't the teamsters who got the news first. They are the worst gossips," Nora says.

"Seriously," adds Kara. "All they ever talk about is who's canoodling who in the vans to and from crew parking."

My stomach tight, my face heating, my first instinct is to flee, but I make myself meet the gazes of the women surrounding me. What I see isn't exactly judgement. Curiosity, for sure. But mostly glee. Since it's now out of my control, I suppose the only thing I can do is face it.

"Let's just be clear. The only important thing is making sure that my social life doesn't distract from the many challenges we face trying to bring this movie in on time with less money. More than ever, I need people to trust and respect me."

I pause for a restorative slug of my drink. "With that in mind, if people ask, yes, Sully and I are dating—even though I hate that word—"

"Well, let's come up with another one," Kara says, in a tone that has enough mischief in it to worry me.

"She's got a point," Glenda says. "If you want your messaging to be on point, you should pick the word."

Gemma clears her throat delicately. "In that case, I'm afraid we're going to need a few more specifics. If you want our help, that is."

Before I can say yea or nay, Nora jumps in. "Like, is this like a friends-with-benefits thing? Just an occasional booty call? Or is he your boo?"

"Um, not the first or the second. It's more… we are closer than that. But I don't know what a 'boo' is."

"I think it's kind of the equivalent to 'beau.'" Glenda taps her chin thoughtfully. "Didn't you say he made you a mix CD?"

"Oooh." Nora rubs her hands together. "You're way beyond just hooking up."

Sherry leans across the table and pins me with a look. "Are you sure the *only* important thing is making sure the shoot goes smoothly?"

I flop back into my chair, hands up. "Fine. I really like the guy, okay? But we have a serious challenge ahead of us when we start back up Monday. People could be ready to hit the ground running, or they could drag their feet out of resentment. And it's my job—*our* job—to push, prod, cheerlead, whatever it takes, to get people back on board. If we don't, the show is fucked, and who I'm fucking really doesn't matter."

The other women slump back into their chairs practically as one.

After a few beats of silence, Glenda clears her throat. "Here's what I think we should do. We"—drawing a circle, she catches the eye of every woman at the table—"contain it. If someone starts yammering on about Helen and Sully, we shut it down by calmly and directly asking why it's any of their business. If anyone has a problem with how they're doing their job, we invite them to either talk to Helen directly or share specifics so we can do so on their behalf. Then we remind them of how hard Helen worked to keep every single person on staff despite her superiors wanting to make cuts."

Her suggestion is greeted with a chorus of assent.

"I like it."

"Sounds good to me."

"On it, boss."

Weirdly, I find myself with a throat clogged with emotion. "Thanks, guys, I… just, thank you."

I'm more than grateful that Glenda and crew have my back, but once I'm back in my apartment, alone except for the cat, fear creeps in again.

Along with its best friend dread.

When everything imploded at Movomax, when Arnie—my older, successful, powerful boss—cut me loose after a two-year affair, it wasn't just my heart that was broken. My career took a major hit. The slimeball offered to set me up with another job in return for my silence. Since I didn't want his help, when I moved out west, I had to basically start over from scratch.

And even though I stayed mum about it all, anyway,

meaning that his wife didn't find out that he'd stepped out on her, everyone at the office knew. The looks of pity and derision and disgust—even from people I thought were friends—still fill me with shame more than ten years later.

Mr. Jones bumps my forearm, forcing me to loosen my grip on the back of the couch. Stroking his back as he arches into my touch helps to slow the spin of my thoughts and the race of my heart.

*You are not Arnie,* some deep part of me whispers. *You would never do any of the things he did.*

With that in mind, does it matter that people are talking about us?

Unfortunately, yes.

The idea of facing them head-on, following Glenda's plan, has my dinner churning in my gut.

I just don't think I have a choice.

## SULLY

Once the trick-or-treaters have dwindled down to high schoolers looking for handouts without bothering to don costumes, I head into the kitchen to do a bit of cleanup, and then, despite not being invited, I head over to Helen's.

Her car's in the parking lot and her lights are on, but even though I have a key, it feels weird to just walk in. Pretty sure she gave it to me just so I can check on the cat and make her dinner and close up if I leave after she does in the morning—which has been happening more often than not.

When I knock, however, there's no answer. Pressing my ear to the door, I think I hear voices inside.

After a few moments of standing there feeling like an idiot, I knock again, louder. Just when I'm about to give up, the door opens and two eyeballs—one human, one feline—peer through the tiny crack the chain allows.

"Jeez, Sully," Helen says. "You scared the crap out of me."

"Sorry. Also for coming over unannounced. I just—I forgot to ask you to keep Mr. Jones inside. Because of Halloween and he's a black cat… Anyway, obviously, he's okay."

I'm babbling, she's just standing there looking all sexy and disheveled, her lips redder than I'm used to, but the chain still hangs between us. "But hey, I know you wanted a little space tonight, so I'll, uh… get out of your hair."

Before I can turn around, the door shuts, the chain clanks against it, the door opens again, and an arm shoots out to haul me inside.

What I see before me is a waaay different O'Neill than I'm used to. I mean, she's always sexy, but with heels and a short skirt making her legs look miles long and a top that dips low to serve up some serious cleavage… I'm speechless.

I don't get much time to enjoy the view, however, because she's pulling me toward the couch. "I'm so glad you came over. I turned on the TV just in time to see a guy get slaughtered in his bed by Freddy Krueger. It got me so freaked out I was afraid to go into my bedroom, let alone go to sleep.

"When I switched the channel, *Halloween* was on, and the guy in the sheet was strangling the girl on the phone. Then I couldn't even call you and ask you to come over."

"Because you might suffer the same fate?" I'm on the verge of laughing at her, but I won't, because my imagination works the same way. Then my brain takes in what's happening on the screen now. "*Misery*? You're not getting any ideas, are you?"

She releases my hand and hurries over to turn off the television, before returning to tug me toward her bedroom.

When I resist, *she* laughs at *me*. "You seriously think I need a sledgehammer to keep you in my bed?"

I shake my head, but instead of following, I let go of her

hand and step back, giving myself a moment to enjoy the view again.

One dark brow arches. One side of her crimson mouth lifts. “What? You don’t like my sexy boss costume?”

I have no words in response to that question.

Only action will suffice.

# CHAPTER 24

> "Annie, when you're attracted to someone, it just means that your subconscious is attracted to their subconscious, subconsciously. So what we think of as fate is just two neuroses knowing that they are a perfect match."
>
> —*Sleepless in Seattle*

## SULLY

MONDAY MORNING, Helen gathers everyone in our small department for a meeting after John arrives and before Dee heads out. She thanks us for our patience and flexibility regarding the unplanned hiatus, then dives into the nitty-gritty.

"Every single department has tightened belts so we can get this movie made with the money we've got, but we're the ones who have to hold the line on those cuts."

She paces back and forth at the front of the room, her presence commanding our attention. All I can think is, if I ever had a teacher with her passion, I'd have paid a hell of a lot more attention in school.

"We have to be on top of every receipt coming into this office," she continues, writing *New Rules* on the whiteboard next to the production calendar, where they'll be visible for anyone who enters to see. "There's not a penny to spare. If it's not already a line item, it's not going to get paid. I've made that clear to all the department heads, but I need you to know that I mean it."

"If a department overspends, the balance comes out of their budget. They've got to make it up. There is no slush fund." She writes the words *Petty Cash,* an equal sign and a big zero on the board and then turns to face us. "That includes overtime, and that includes this office."

John raises his hand. "What if we still have work to do when our ten hours are up?"

"Fifteen minutes before your day ends, bring what's unfinished to me. I'm not hourly, so I don't get overtime. I'll stay till it's done."

"Maybe we could stagger our schedules even more so someone's here," Dee says. "Like, in case you need to be on set."

"I could come in later," John says.

"And I can't stay later, but I could come in earlier. Hmm. Then my husband would have to get the kids to school and daycare in the morning." Dee presses her hands together in prayer. "Please, please, Helen, make me come in earlier."

Helen shakes her head, but she laughs.

"I'm not even kidding, Helen. Those babies are monsters in the morning."

I raise my hand, something I never did in school. "I could clock out in the middle of the day for a couple hours, then clock in and stay later."

Helen takes in a deep breath and lets it out again, like this went better than she'd expected. "Thanks, guys. I truly appreciate the offers. I'm probably going to have to be on set at lunch and the end of the day to make sure meal penalties and overtime aren't slipping in, so having the office covered could be helpful."

John leans back in his chair and grunts. "Maybe just get that second AD a watch that works."

"Seriously," Dee says with a roll of her eyes.

"Okay. Good meeting." Helen claps her hands. "Let's get to work. We'll start the new schedule tomorrow. And again, thank you for your flexibility."

John waves her gratitude down. "It's all good, boss."

Helen heads for her office but then pauses to speak from the doorway. "Oh, and one more thing. Sully and I are currently in a relationship. It should not affect what happens in this office, where we plan to behave professionally. The department heads know to ward off gossip. If you have an issue with the situation, please speak with me directly."

She waits until both John and Dee utter a somewhat surprised "Okay" before disappearing into her office.

Where I follow, moving so quickly I almost trip on my way through the door. After closing it behind me, I hiss, "You could have given me a heads-up before sharing that with everyone."

She looks up from sifting through papers on her desk, a crease in her brow. "I thought that's what you wanted."

"Yeah, but it makes me feel like, I don't know"—my hands flail at my sides—"lesser than you if you're the one telling everyone, and it's obvious I didn't even know it was coming. That was embarrassing, Helen."

"In this office, I'm your boss. It was an executive decision. I don't want speculation about us to be a distraction if and when people see us together." She crosses her arms over her chest. "Tongues are already wagging, you know."

Hand in the air, I nod. "I get it. In future, though, if you're going to share information that involves me, I'd appreciate a little advance warning."

She nods sharply. "Fair enough."

Then she just shifts into work mode, making lists and barking orders.

This new reality is going to take a little getting used to.

## HELEN

I'll never say any of it out loud; I'm afraid to even think it because it might tempt the gods to fuck with my good fortune, but the last few weeks of principal photography for *Hacked* turn out to be the easiest I've ever managed. It could've gone either way. Diva fits could've been thrown right and left. But instead, from the executive producers down to the lowliest PAs, everyone has pulled together.

Maybe it's the fact that people truly like this director, and it wasn't anyone's fault that his appendix blew, but I'd like to think it comes down to good leadership. My crew chiefs set the bar, and people stepped up.

I have to admit that my mood's been enhanced by the presence of a certain man in my life. From the shoulder massages at the end of the day, to the coffee in bed in the morning, the man is spoiling me rotten.

A girl could get used to this life.

If only she could figure out a way for it to continue.

Right now, though, this girl has got work to do. My eyes are crossing from staring at the computer screen for so long, so I decide to print out the day's hot costs so I can stare at paper instead as I proof and edit them.

As the pages spit out of the Xerox machine, my stomach grumbles. In the olden days, I'd have a cigarette to stay alert. I'm thinking I might have to visit craft service for a snack to power me through the final hours of the workday, when I hear a familiar voice calling my name.

Stepping out into the hallway, it's a pleasant surprise to see Dani Goodwin and her friend Violet in our office doorway. "Looking for me?"

"Yes, ma'am," Dani says.

"Hang on, I'll be there in a sec," I call, grabbing the print-outs from the machine, before returning to meet them in the hall. "To what do I owe the pleasure?"

Violet lifts a bag. "We heard you had to work late again, so we bring treats."

I narrow my eyes at them. "And who told you I was working late?"

Dani shrugs. "A little bird."

"A big bird is more like it," I mutter. When they don't follow me inside, I say, "Well, don't just stand there. Come on in and show me what you've got."

"Eggrolls," Violet says, setting a takeout container on Sully's desk. The tantalizing combination of ginger, soy sauce, and sesame fill the air, and my stomach growls so loudly that Dani laughs.

"Guess we got here just in time."

"You said it. Lunch was a long time ago." I dip a warm eggroll into what looks like sweet-and-sour sauce and take a bite. "Oh, that's good. I didn't think Wallington had an Asian restaurant."

"It ain't as fancy as what you'd have in LA, but it usually hits the spot," Dani says before taking a bite herself.

As we eat, they ask me about our show's progress before filling me in on what they've been up to.

"And it's not just actors," Violet continues, describing the growth to her casting business. "More and more crew people are choosing to move to Wallington after working here. Nate—my boyfriend—expected his stay to be short-term, but now he's moved here. Same for the cinematographer, the best boy, and the key grip on *Lawson's Reach*."

"Well, that makes sense when you're working on a show that shoots eight or nine months out of the year. But if you're working features, you have to be in LA to get the next job," I point out.

"Even if you're as well established as you are?" Dani asks. Her tone is mildly curious, but something tells me that these two aren't here just to bring me snacks.

"Did Sully sic you on me?"

Violet spreads a hand over her ample bosom and gasps theatrically. "I don't know what you're talking about."

"Way to be obvious, Vi." Dani swats at her before turning to me. "He did not. We are here of our own accord to try and convince you to give Wallington a chance. We could use more kickass women around here."

"Agreed," Violet says. "And speaking of the next job, something's in the wind about a shakeup to come on *Lawson's Reach*. Above the line. Like way above."

"The showrunner?"

Violet tips her head back and forth. "Nothing confirmed, but yes. I also heard that the resulting shuffle could put the LP in the EP job, which would mean they'd need a line producer."

I have been itching to move up into that position on a bigger job, but what I say is, "I don't know. I try to stay away from TV."

"Why? Wouldn't it be nice to know you had the regular work?"

"But then that's what it becomes. Regular work. Instead of a carney going to a new place with every project, pitching my tent, and working with new people, I'd be a drone at a regular old nine-to-five." I shudder. "Between that and having to maintain this kind of schedule for nine months of the year… no thank you."

I can tell that my reaction isn't at all what they were hoping for, and when I hint that I do need to finish up my reports for the day, they bustle around cleaning up the mess.

On the way out the door, though, Dani throws out one last shot. "Sully's pretty special. He might be worth bending your rules."

Instead of arguing that I've already done that, that maybe the man himself should be asking me to stick around if that's what he really wants, I just shoo them out of the office, so I can be alone.

With my work *and* my worries.

# CHAPTER 25

"You're not perfect, sport, and let me save you the suspense: this girl you've met, she's not perfect either. But the question is whether or not you're perfect for each other."

—*Good Will Hunting*

## HELEN

AFTER A LATE LUNCH/EARLY dinner on a Sunday, Sully asks if I want to go to the beach.

"In November?"

"Unless the wind is blowing sideways and pelting you with sand, I'll take the beach any day of the year," he argues. "Plus, walking in the sand is good therapy for me."

I can't say no to that, so we bundle up and head out before we lose the light. His car is blocking mine so he offers to drive. When he starts it up, a cassette begins to play on the car radio, a man speaking quietly and deliberately, in an accent I can't quite identify.

Before I can ask what it is, Sully turns it off and turns on the CD player instead. As Pearl Jam's "Better Man" comes over the speakers, I ask, "What was that tape playing before? Or *who* was it?"

Sully stretches his arm across the back of my seat and turns around to back out of the driveway. "Oh, it's just something I listen to a little bit every day."

"But what is it?"

"His name is Thich Nhat Hanh, and he's, like, a Buddhist teacher."

"Are you Buddhist?"

"Not really." He tips his head side to side, considering as he pulls out onto the street. "I mean, he uses the word god every once in a while, but it doesn't seem like the kind of religion my friends grew up with. It's more like tips for living."

"What made you start listening to it?"

"Dani brought home a whole bag of New Age-y tapes when she cleaned out some actor's apartment at the end of a production last spring. She offered to mail them to him but he said the fact that he left them was 'meant to be and the universe wanted her to have them.'" He makes his voice sound spaced out as he quotes the guy, but something tells me he takes this seriously.

"Interesting. How come you have them?"

He laughs. "Dani thought that idea was ridiculous. They were just lying around the house, so I took some with me on the boat. Figured I might learn something."

I adjust my seat so it's leaning back a bit and take in the houses as we drive by. As we leave my neighborhood of big old homes from the turn of the century to head toward Wrightsboro beach, the homes get smaller. "People leave behind weird things, huh?"

"Mostly messes, she says."

"Guys are pretty messy."

"She says the women are just as bad, if not worse. Everything from pots put away without being washed to makeup stains on towels."

"Actresses." I groan. "Pains in the asses."

"Actually, actors *and* actresses leave makeup stains."

"Guess that makes sense."

He shrugs. "Some people leave a place better than how they found it; some people leave a mess."

I look over to study his profile. "Which are you?"

"I try to be the former."

"Hm." I take in the floor of his car, which is littered with sand and bits of trash. "Your car's a mess."

"Yeah." He shoots me an unrepentant look. "Nobody's perfect."

"Good to know. I was worried."

Eyes back on the road, he adds, "Except… maybe I'm perfect for you."

I don't answer, but something occurs to me. Sully is extraordinarily patient, a quality I lack. Maybe this guru of his could be good for me. After I pull the cassette tape out to examine it, I can't help but laugh when I read its title. "Sully! This is for walking meditation."

"Yep."

"That seems cruelly ironic. Or frustrating, at the very least."

He shrugs. "It was what I pulled out of the bag, so I guess that's what the universe wanted me to hear. Anyway, I think the point is that you can meditate anytime, anywhere."

"I'm going to play it if that's okay."

"Suit yourself," he says, but his smile belies his words.

As the view out the car window shifts again, from grassy wetlands to a set of grand homes with views of the intracoastal, we listen. I'm not sure I understand exactly what the guy means by the past being alive in the present, but there's something about his voice that's comforting.

After Sully parks in a deserted parking lot close to a path through the dunes and turns off the car, I actually feel a little bereft.

I'm still turning the monk's words over when we leave the asphalt behind. When Sully stops to remove his shoes, I almost bump into him. "A little cold to go barefoot, don't you think?"

"Veronica suggested using the sand to work my feet. I have to stay mindful so that I use the muscles properly."

I'd never heard the word "mindful" before the Buddhist guy said it, and now Sully's just tossing it around.

"So, do you actually meditate?"

"Not very well." His mouth quirks. "But I guess that's not the point. What I mean is, I don't sit down and meditate every day, especially with the schedule my current boss has me working—"

"Watch it there, mister."

He just laughs and then drapes an arm over my shoulders to hug me into his side. "Seriously, though. Like he says, it's not just about sitting. Anytime I'm alone—driving, working out, cooking—I try to remember to be present."

"Was it just happening on these tapes that got you into it? Or had you, like, studied Eastern philosophy or something in school?"

"I think I've always been drawn to that way of being in the world, but I didn't know much about it. My parents aren't religious." He glances over, and his smile is as open and beautiful as I've ever seen it. "The beach and the water have always been my church."

He pauses to point out a swarm of wet-suited surfers. "Out on the waves, there's no agenda. Well, sometimes there's competition to learn a trick, something like that. But for me, I got a high like nothing else when I'd let myself just be the wave. Let the wind and the current and the power of the water move me."

The longing in his voice is heartbreaking, so I encircle his waist and give him a squeeze. "I would've thought it'd be about how you handle your body and the surfboard."

"It's the opposite. You can't control all that." His free hand sweeps over the horizon. "You respect her. You let her cradle you."

"Was it the same on the boat?"

"Yeah." He nods slowly. "Once I was able to let go of all the reasons I left, anyway. Every decision became simple. Where to go, when to eat. When to move, when to be still."

"Sounds like you found enlightenment."

He barks out a laugh as he shifts our path so that we're walking parallel to the water's edge. "I was nowhere near it. I'd still get frustrated, make mistakes. But the moments where I was in sync were like heaven. In fact, I'd had a perfect day right before I got hit."

I rest my head on his shoulder and watch his feet move through the sand, noting that there's hardly a difference between the right and left. "Tell me about it. If you want to."

He squints into the distance for a few moments before he speaks, like he has to prepare himself. But his voice is calm as he describes what does sound like a peaceful day. Perfect, right up until the moment he got hit.

"I've thought a lot about that day. Like, if I hadn't rowed ashore and interacted with that family, they might not have been so quick to pull the boat to shore. They were nice people, I'm sure they would've called 911. But because we'd met, I think they worked a little harder to make sure I was okay."

"You have a lot more faith in people than I do."

The light is waning, so we turn around to walk back to the car. We listen to the tape again on the way back, and when he parks in front of my place, I ask, "Do you have any more of these?"

"Why? You want to keep listening?"

"Yeah. Why not?"

"You going to use it to get you pumped for work instead of Blind Melon?"

"I could try it. Maybe I'd be more zen."

"No more reducing assistants to tears? You'll be all, 'This is just a feeling that I do not need to act upon'?"

"Fuck no. I'm still going to yell at people. But I'll be calmer afterwards."

## SULLY

A couple weeks into the rebooted production schedule, Helen calls me into her office right after John leaves for the day.

"What can I do you for, boss? Or is this just my daily notice that I'm fired?"

I've been joking that she can lay me off each and every day as long as that means I *get* laid.

She rolls her eyes. "If that's what it takes. But I wanted to talk to you about a different hiatus."

This has me dropping into a chair. "Are we shutting down again?"

"No, no. Sorry. I mean Thanksgiving."

"Ohhh, gotcha."

"Since we have a four-day weekend, I was wondering if you'd like to take a trip? We could go to Charleston, or Asheville, even Bermuda if you want."

There's something about Helen's desire to travel. Like, it's more about wanting to escape than about wanting to go somewhere. But that's not why I say no. "Sorry, but I've already promised my mom that I'd be home for Thanksgiving dinner. My brother and his new baby are coming, plus a stray grad student or two from the university."

Her disappointment is clear, but it's hard to tell if it's because I can't go away, or because I didn't invite her to my family's gathering, so I add, "You're totally welcome to join us. There's always room for more. I just figured you'd be doing dinner with Glenda and them."

"Thanks, but if I stay in town, I do plan on dinner with the girls." She turns her attention to her computer screen, but adds, "We could still leave Friday morning."

"I really can't. My friends always have a Black Friday party."

"Okay, well, just thought I'd ask."

"You should come to the party. It'll be fun. Games and hanging out and eating leftovers."

"I'll think about it." She begins to type something, then pauses and meets my questioning gaze. "That's it. You can go."

Instead of doing as she suggests, I lean forward, resting my forearms on my thighs. "Helen. Are you mad that I didn't invite you to these things earlier?"

"No." She waves a dismissive hand in the air. "I mean, you've got your traditions or whatever…"

"That doesn't mean you can't be a part of them. Traditions evolve. I mean, Vi's family doesn't own the inn where we've always had the party, but we're doing it anyway."

"I'm not going to intrude on your family and friends."

"If you're invited, you're not intruding."

"You're just asking me because you feel sorry for the poor old lady who doesn't have a family of her own."

"I'm asking because I want to spend time with you. I want you to be a part of my life." Her eyes are still glued to the monitor, but she's clicking the mouse like she's just using it to avoid me. "Helen, please look at me."

When she does, her face is so carefully blank that it makes me want to scream. Instead, I say, "I get it if you don't want to continue this conversation now but can we do it later? At your place?"

She nods and *then* turns back to the computer.

I guess I have to take it as a win.

## HELEN

For the first time since we returned to Wallington from Virginia, I'm not looking forward to having Sully waiting for me back at my apartment. Even when I walk in the door to the aromas of yet another home-cooked gourmet meal, my gut tightens with anxiety.

I'm too hungry to let my concerns keep me from devouring every bite of the sauteed local flounder with a caper and butter sauce alongside roasted winter vegetables. But after we've finished the dishes and collapsed onto the couch, where Sully takes my feet in his to give them a massage, the words fairly burst out of me.

"Okay, okay. I'm sorry that I gave you the cold shoulder earlier. There are just so many unknowns that it's making me crazy."

He nods slowly, his thumbs doing something magical to the backs of my heels. "I get it."

"And, yes, I was a little hurt that you hadn't asked me to join you for Thanksgiving and the… the Black Friday thing or whatever, but at the same time, getting introduced to your parents as your girlfriend? When we don't even know what's happening with us a month from now? Why go through all the drama, you know?"

His calm just winds me up even more, so I pull my feet away from him and get up to pace. "Those tapes you listen to —are they why you're not pushing me for… I don't know, a definition of what's going on between us?"

"Like a commitment?"

"I guess." Before he can elaborate further, I move on to another of my worries. "On the other hand, aren't you afraid of being hurt? When this ends?"

A shadow crosses his face, but it's quickly replaced by something that's not quite serenity, not quite resignation. "Of course I am. But life is about suffering and how you deal with it. You can't escape it."

"You're saying I cause you to suffer?

"You did, when I wanted you and I couldn't have you. Once I'd had a taste, it was clear that I'd rather have what I can with you than give you up to avoid some possible future suffering."

"Does that mean you're willing to give this up? When the show ends?"

"I'm not saying that. Far from it. I've never felt about anyone the way I feel about you."

He shrugs, like that solves everything, which just pisses me off. "Because you're a baby. You haven't lived long enough."

"Have you?" he lobs right back, his tone still infuriatingly calm.

"Have I what?"

"Felt like this before?"

"It's irrelevant."

"How is it irrelevant? Every day I wake up next to you, I feel lucky that I get to spend another day with you."

"How about today? How's that going for you?"

He pauses for a moment, then nods. "You challenge me. You don't let me sit around and feel sorry for myself."

"Your friends do the same."

"My friends don't make every one of my nerve cells feel things more. Things taste better, colors are brighter."

"That could be attributed to your life-threatening accident."

"Maybe. Or maybe everything would be worse." He grabs my hand, forcing me to stop moving, squeezes it once, and lets it go. "Listen, O'Neill. It was obvious from the moment I met you that no one's going to ever make you do something you don't want to. I know because I'm the same. I'm just quieter about it."

I frown, not quite sure I get where he's going with this.

"Instead of trying to pin you down…" He bites his lip, like he's not sure he wants to continue.

But I know this game, and I can wait. Which I do, brows up.

His cheeks go pink, and he finally spits it out. "Instead, I've been doing my best to woo you."

I narrow my eyes at him. "Like, manipulate me?"

"No, woo. Court. Romance."

"Like when you cook for me, bring me treats, give me hundreds of orgasms…"

"I'm just doing my best to make your life easier, so we can enjoy the time we have more fully."

I'm sure any other woman would be a puddle at the feet of this superman, but I can't let go of the idea that he's buttering me up for the kill. After all, Arnie spent many hours and thousands of dollars charming me, cosseting me, coddling me. Until he cut me loose.

So instead of giving in, I switch tacks. "I got a call today after you left about a job in Chicago. If you don't want this to end, you could come with me. Not the ideal time to be in the city, but it's a great restaurant town."

"What, just tag along and be your love slave?"

"Well, that, and work with me." I drop onto the couch next to him. "Come on, it'll be fun. We're a great team."

He takes a deep breath before replying. "Helen, I appreciate you hiring me when I had no experience as an assistant. You got me off the couch. But by January, I'm going to be strong enough to work on my feet again. I can't spend my life in the office."

"Not even for me?" Despite my attempt to keep my tone light, there's a brittleness to it that I hate.

"It's not the work itself, or who I'm working for," he adds, but his tone isn't teasing; it's too, too serious. "I need to get my hours back up so I don't lose my health insurance. And as you know, compared to what I'd be getting as a utility guy in the sound department, this pay sucks."

"I could probably get you a better rate on the next job, now that I've trained you up," I add, trying my damnedest to get this conversation going how I want it.

"I need an IATSE job, Helen. PAs aren't covered by the union."

"Then we'll find you one."

"Helen, are you really going to hire a sound mixer and then tell the guy he can't use his usual third man because your boyfriend needs a job?"

He's right, of course he is, but that doesn't mean I have to like it.

# CHAPTER 26

"When we live in the spirit of gratitude, there will be much happiness in our life. The one who is grateful is the one who has much happiness while the one who is ungrateful will not be able to have happiness."

—Thich Nhat Hanh

## HELEN

I DON'T HAVE Thanksgiving dinner with Sully's family, but I do stop by for dessert. He introduces me to his family as his boss, which I dislike way more than I'll ever admit.

Theirs is a cozy little house, the perfect combination of clean and messy, filled with the scents of home-cooked food that they apparently made as a group, and lots of laughter. As I'd imagined, his home and his parents are idyllic compared to the circumstances I grew up in. To top it all off, Sully's a natural with his niece and nephew, playing with the three-year-old like he actually enjoys *Chutes and Ladders,* and making faces with the baby until it laughs.

Meanwhile, I'm mostly thankful that there are so many people present, I can just blend into the woodwork, which is about all I can handle as the clock ticks down on whatever this is between me and Mr. Calloway.

I also go to the game night on Friday. It's a little awkward when Sully stumbles over what to call me, as some of the people seem to know we're together while some don't. Once we get past the introductions, however, I actually have fun. The only game we played in my house growing up was called "Don't Make Daddy Mad" or "Pretend Mommy's Not Dying." After I moved out, I had no time for games.

People seem surprised when I don't know the rules to *Yahtzee* or *Clue* or *Boggle*, but no one asks why; they just tell me the rules. By the end of the night, I feel like a kid. Like the kid I never was, maybe. Which makes me happy and terribly sad all at the same time.

Over the rest of the long weekend, Sully and I spend the time we're not eating or making love going for walks. We don't talk much; we don't address the future. We just walk. Together.

Every day feels like a gift, even though the thought of leaving makes me so sad I can't even look at my calendar past the day we're to close the production office. When I'm alone and not working, I'm listening to the Buddhist, who turns out to be a Vietnamese guy who has survived a great deal of suffering. Which does put a little perspective on my own troubles.

I have to spend the Sunday evening of Thanksgiving weekend catching up on work, but I do it at my apartment. Sully comes over, builds a fire in the fireplace, and Mr. Jones snuggles next to me in the armchair as I go over the schedule for the last full week of shooting.

When we sit down to eat, I raise my glass. "Thank you. For not listening to me."

He clinks my wine with his. "Back atcha, boss."

It's not until we've finished the dishes and are curled up on the couch together that I gather my courage. "So, I have a question for you. I want you to know that this is different than when I asked you to go out of town this weekend. And it's not about trying to convince you to go to Chicago with me."

He puts down the book he's been reading. "I'm listening."

"There's a thing I should go to in a few weeks, a DGA event. It's a schmooze-fest, you know, a way to get facetime with producers and directors. The thing is, it's in New York, and... I don't like to go there on my own."

His brows come together. "But I thought New York is a lot safer now."

"It is. For most people. And it's not that I'm truly frightened, but..." I swallow past the bile rising in my throat. "Growing up, my dad was abusive."

"He hit you?"

I nod slowly, hanging on to calm by a thread. "Mostly my mom, but occasionally me. Mostly when he was drunk. Every time my mom threatened to leave him, he'd cry and promise to never do it again and shower her with presents we couldn't afford. But he'd always start drinking again, and the cycle would start right back up. And then one day she found out she had cancer that had already spread through her entire—"

A sob surprises me and I fight it back, but Sully's got me in his lap and in his arms before I can take another breath.

"I'm so sorry, Helen."

"It's fine. I'm fine," I protest, even as the tears on my cheeks and snot in my nose make me a liar. "It was a long time ago."

It takes a minute to wrest back control, but I do. "Anyway, the point is, I still hate the bastard, and I have this unreasonable fear of being in the city. I haven't been able to get anyone else to go so—"

"Of course I'll go with you," he answers before I can even ask.

"You'd have to wear a suit, but if you don't have one, I'm sure Sherry can help you out with something from her stock."

He doesn't seem bothered by the details, but I have to ask again. "You sure you don't mind? Don't feel obligated or anything."

I bite my lip hard as I wait for his answer, but he doesn't leave me hanging.

"I would be honored to accompany you, O'Neill."

## HELEN

As is our tradition, Glenda and I meet for Sunday brunch the final week of the show. After the wrap party, but before the wrap-out days when the crew gets packed up and actually leaves town, a little celebration always helps me to power through the often sad and always irksome tasks of closing a production down.

"To another show."

After we clink glasses and take a sip of the delicious bottle of bubbly, she asks, "So, where do you go from here?"

"That's the million-dollar question, isn't it? To another UPM gig or hold out for a Line Producer job." I lift my glass again before realizing that Glenda's never said anything about doing anything other being a coordinator. "What about you? Do you ever think about moving up?"

Her expression is more grimace than smile. "To what, producer? Ugh. I don't want to have to risk other people's money. And I hate schmoozing."

"But there's still the schmoozing to get the work."

"That's why I got an agent. I let her do that crap." She refills our nearly empty flutes. "You know, you should talk to her. If all the kickass women go to her, it'll be like a rising tide."

"Maybe. I do feel like I've been blindly climbing a ladder without knowing why or where I'm going."

"Like Jack and the Beanstalk?" she asks. "What's behind the clouds: gold or a giant?"

"More like I'm afraid if I stop that it'll disappear."

The waiter arrives with our food, and after we dig in, Glenda says, "When I asked what was next, though, I meant for the holidays."

"Oh, right." I shake my head. "Honestly, I'm not sure. This damn job has taken every bit of my concentration the past few weeks."

"I don't know," Glenda says, dragging out the vowels of the last word. "Seems like you've had something else—or someone else—to concentrate on."

Glenda, like everyone on the show, really, has been exceptionally good about Sully and me: no teasing, no innuendos. So I can give a little bit. "I have, and I've enjoyed the… stress relief, shall we say, immensely."

This gets a laugh, and I take the opportunity to shine the light back on her. "What about you? Any big holiday plans?"

She nods as she finishes chewing a bite of croissant and wipes her mouth with the fancy cloth napkin. "Me and the hubs are going to Hawaii for the holidays. Hikes in volcanos, drinks on the beach, the whole bit."

"Haven't you had enough of the beach?"

"Eh, I'm like you—can't really relax when I'm on the job. And it's not as fun without Tim."

"When are you going?"

She spears a chunk of pineapple. "Two days after I get back. Can. Not. Wait."

"Sounds perfect." I fill my mouth with food as I try to figure out how to ask what I really want to ask. "So, what is this? Our fifth together?"

"Let's see." She counts on her fingers. "There were three

forgettable movies of the week, then *Mars Attacks,* then *Leaving Las Vegas,* so actually, this is number six."

I point my fork at her. "You were my date to the Indie Spirit Awards for that last one."

"Right. Tim couldn't make it back from… I think he was in London."

"So"—I clear my throat, not expecting to get an opening so quickly—"I have a question about that, actually."

"London? You have a project coming up there?"

"Uh, not that I know of. No, I wanted to ask about your marriage."

She raises a brow and takes a sip of champagne. "Go on."

"I mean, not the dirty details, of course. I just—I've always wondered how you two do it. How you manage to stay together when you're never… together."

She laughs. "Honey, that *is* how we stay together."

"I mean, you have to admit, it's hardly typical."

She settles back into the worn armchair, crosses her legs, and gazes out the large plate glass windows. She's a beautiful woman, despite—or perhaps because of—the laugh lines around her eyes and mouth. "You're right, but I think more couples would enjoy it if they had the opportunity. We each have independent, interesting careers. When we're together, we're often on a break, so we can just have fun. I don't think it would work if we didn't make each other laugh, though."

"All that time apart, though. Do you ever"—I know it's rude of me to ask, but I can't help myself—"stray?"

"I don't know if he has. I did, once."

She says this so matter-of-factly that I press further. "And it was okay with him?"

She shakes her head. "I didn't tell him. Never will."

"That doesn't weigh on you?"

She sets her drink down. "All I can say is, trust is the most important thing."

"But you lied to him. Isn't that a violation of trust?"

She opens her mouth but before she can rebut, I add, "I'm not judging. I just don't understand."

She nods. "I appreciate that clarification, but we talked this all through before we got married. We'd both been around the block a few times, if you know what I mean. Both been married before, much too young. Both well into our careers. Met on the job but knew that there was no way we'd work together all the time."

"What does he do again?"

"Best boy."

"Mm. You're hired by completely different departments."

"Exactly. And we never have worked together again." She shrugs. "Just hasn't worked out. Anyway, before we got married, we made a set of rules."

Since production coordinators are as detail-oriented and control freaky as UPMs, if not more so, this doesn't surprise me.

She holds up a finger. "Rule one: if we slept with someone else when we were out on the road and we knew right away it was a mistake, that there was no emotional connection, we'd never tell."

"And that's what happened to you?"

"I'd had a bad day, I met a cute traveling salesman at a bar, and we had sex. Never saw him again." Her nose wrinkles in distaste. "Wasn't much fun, either."

"And the other rules?"

"If we started to develop an infatuation with someone or thought we were falling in love, we had to tell right away."

"Has that happened?"

"To Tim. Twice." She rests an elbow on the table and runs a hand through her hair. "It wasn't easy, but we worked through it. Both times, it was clear that it was about other crap. He was upset about his dad dying, and then he was having a hard time with the gaffer he was working with and needed support."

"What happened?" I can't believe she's sharing so much, but I can't stop asking either. It's more fascinating than the script of any movie I've ever worked on.

She looks out the windows of the beachfront restaurant. "It wasn't easy. He got pretty attached to this young script supervisor."

"I can't believe how mature you are about all this."

She laughs. "Oh, I wasn't very mature at the time. Luckily, I'd just finished up a job, and I flew out to see him on location in Boston. We fought it out and figured it out."

She picks at the remains of her omelet with her fork before setting it down again. "We chose the marriage. You have to choose to stay married, choose to value it. We don't have kids, so it's always a choice. And that means a lot."

I sit back in my own chair to contemplate her story. "Whenever people find out that I'm not married, they ask, 'Aren't you lonely?'"

Glenda nods. "My family asks the same thing. 'Don't I miss Tim when he's gone or when I'm on location?' They just don't get how all-absorbing our work is. And most of them don't know what's it's like when you're not working. How that can be great, but also nerve-racking when you don't know when the next job will come. That's when it's nice to be with a partner who's in the same boat."

I never imagined I'd find such a partner. No one I ever worked with seemed like someone worth trusting in that way.

Until now.

# CHAPTER 27

"When you love someone, you have to have trust and confidence. Love without trust is not yet love."

—Thich Nhat Hanh, *How to Love*

## SULLY

THE LAST WEEK of production is a whirlwind, and Helen doesn't slow down even after production ends. She makes a brief appearance at the wrap party, but is back at the office later that night, working with Glenda to keep tabs on the return of rental equipment, the cleaning of housing, and the never-ending collection of walkie-talkies, which, according to her, must have legs of their own because you can never track down every single one.

I've had dinner waiting for a couple of hours by the time she drags herself into the apartment the night before she flies back to California.

"Well?" After she hangs up her coat, I hand her a glass of red wine. "Are we celebrating or drowning sorrows?"

She clinks her glass with mine and takes an appreciative

sip before answering. "If you're talking about the budget, I'm celebrating that it's done."

"We went over?" I've become as invested as she is in this outcome, and I'll be disappointed if all of our cost-saving measures were for naught.

A slow smile spreads across her face, and she taps my glass again. "I'm just messing with you. Receipts are accounted for, books are balanced, and we came in fifteen dollars under budget."

"You little minx. You may have to pay for teasing me like that."

"Promises, promises," she says in a tone I can't quite read.

"Oh, I can deliver on that promise," I say, taking her wine glass and setting both on the console table by the door.

She laughs. "What're you going to do? *Tie Me Up, Tie Me Down*?"

Hoping that my leg cooperates, I scoop her into my arms and head for her bedroom. "Never saw the movie, but I could improvise."

When we get to the edge of the bed, I ask, "Do I have your permission?"

"To tie me up?"

I nod.

One shoulder lifts. "Maybe. I mean, it kind of freaks me out, giving you that control, but it also sounds kind of... liberating."

"Your wish is my command."

I toss her onto the bed and then point, indicating that she should scoot back. I crawl after her, reveling in the fact that I can put weight on my left shin. We meet at the top of the bed, and I spread her arms wide, my palms flattening hers. As we kiss, my tongue teasing and my teeth nibbling, she tries to hook a leg over my lower back, but I set it back on the bed, casting about in my mind for what I can use to restrain this wildcat. Then I remember the suit hanging in Helen's closet.

When the costume designer pulled it for me, she hung a few ties on its hanger so I'd have a choice depending on the shirt that I used.

Breaking the kiss, I tell Helen to "stay" using the lowest part of my register. "And close your eyes."

After I grab the ties, I strip her of her sensible but fashionable work clothes. Off go the khakis and the pullover sweater and the blouse, leaving her in bra and thong. When she shivers, I command her to be still. "You'll warm up soon enough."

Moving to the end of the bed, I feather a silk tie from the sole of her foot, up her inner leg. I'm rewarded with a rosy flush on her neck and the heightened rise and fall of her chest, budded nipples riding its wave. Continuing the tease, I caress her thigh with the fabric, skate in figure eights from thigh to hip to belly, loving the little gasps that escape from her mouth.

Then I straddle her, pinning her hips with my knees, and slowly tie one wrist and then the other to the bedposts. I notice the sleeping mask on her bedside table and slide it over her eyes, whispering, "Just to make sure."

Only then do I truly begin to have my way with her.

Helen has said multiple times that she can't come without stimulating herself. I've never pushed her on it, but right now seems like the perfect time to prove her wrong. I've had weeks to study her approach, watching the way she circles, slowly at first, moving firmer and faster as she gets closer to climax. Pretty basic technique if you ask me, but since she's the one feeling the build, it makes sense that she knows when to go hard and when to lay off. And I won't deny that the first few times it was hot as hell to see her bring herself to orgasm.

But I'd like to be the one making her lose control for once.

My fingers take the opposite path of the silken tie, skittering down her arms and sides and removing her bra before circling her breasts. Then they find her mouth, brushing her lips apart and encouraging her to suck until my two forefingers are wet. These I drag down the center of her chest and belly, leaving a trail as she arches into the touch. When I get to her mound, I slide off of her, hook my hands under her knees, and pull her toward the foot of the bed until the ties are taut.

After I slide her underwear off, I grab a pillow to cushion my knees, and spread her legs.

"You are so beautiful," I whisper. "Do you trust me, Helen?"

I look up at her face, at teeth now caught on her lower lip, at the chest rising and falling even faster.

"Do you?" I ask again, adding challenge to my tone.

Her buttocks tense in response, so I press her legs even wider apart, spreading my hands across the tops of her thighs.

"Say the word, Helen, and I'll make you come."

"Yes," she whispers, her tone desperate. "Yes, I do. I trust you."

At that, I part her folds, and lower my mouth to feast.

## HELEN

Never have I ever fantasized about being tied up or being dominated. Never would I have pictured slow-moving, gentle Sully taking on such a role. But he is a master at it.

His commanding tone alone sets my nerve endings on fire. The way he tweaks my nipples and slaps my skin takes me right to the edge of pleasure and pain. But it's the brazen way his fingers bare me, the way his tongue and lips devour me that has me putty in his hands. Alternating light flicks with heavy drags, when I can't touch him or see him… it's intoxicating. My hips rise to meet him, greedy for more as every muscle in my body begins to tighten and pulse. When his clever fingers thrust inside and curl upward to tap hard while he sucks deeply with that mouth, I explode. Straining against the ties, hips bucking shamelessly, I'm racked with sensation as I come over and over again.

Then his body covers mine, skin to skin. Either I lost consciousness, or he lost his clothes faster than Superman.

"That was so fucking sexy, Helen," he whispers against my cheek. "*You* are so fucking sexy."

The only words I can manage are. "You. Inside me. Now."

He doesn't argue, but he does untie me and remove the blindfold.

My sight's restored just in time to watch him flop onto his back and roll on a condom. Then his arms stretch wide on the bed, as wide as the grin on his gorgeous face, while a certain part of him stands tall in salute.

Surprised that I have the energy after the electrical circuit overload this man just caused, I lift my chin. "Permission to board, Captain?"

He laughs, his face lit with delight and surprise. "Permission granted."

# CHAPTER 28

"Tragedy blows through your life like a tornado, uprooting everything. Creating chaos. You wait for the dust to settle and then you choose. You can live in the wreckage and pretend it's still the mansion you remember. Or you can crawl from the rubble and slowly rebuild."

—*Can't Hardly Wait*

## SULLY

WHEN I FLY UP to meet her in the Big Apple, Helen and I have been apart for only a week, but the moment I see her in La Guardia airport, I need to be naked with her as soon as is humanly possible.

But first I give her a good long hug.

Taxi drivers in this city must be a hardened lot, because ours doesn't say a thing while we make out in the back seat like teenagers. I'd normally jaw with a hotel desk clerk during check-in, but I barely say a word to the guy, just grab the key and race Helen to the elevator, where we lock lips until the doors slide open on our floor, stumble down the hall in a half embrace looking for the right room, fumble through getting the damn door open, and then find ourselves in the tiniest hotel room I've ever seen in my life.

Not that I've seen so many, but it makes the berth in *Endless Summer* seem spacious.

"Good thing we're friendly," I say after taking it in.

"I'd like to get even friendlier," Helen says. "Right after I pee and hang up my clothes."

Those tasks ticked off the list, things pick right back up where we left them. We strip, eyeing each other as if trying to decide where to start. Then she wraps her arms around my waist and presses her nose into my chest, inhaling deeply.

"I missed your smell."

Busy sliding my palms over her smooth skin, I hear her with only half a mind. "Oh yeah? What do I smell like?"

"Like the ocean. All briny and salty and musky."

"And that's a good thing?"

She looks up, grasps my face with her hands, and whispers, "That is a very good thing."

She's in a hurry, but I want to go slow, so that's what we do. Once we're both sated, I'm starving, but she's yawning.

"I hate taking the red-eye," she mumbles, and within minutes, she's asleep.

The room's too small to do anything that doesn't happen in bed, so I write her a note and head out in search of sustenance. While I'm out, I take a mini-tour of the neighborhood, which includes a quick walk through the southern end of Central Park. By the time I get back, she's awake and hungry.

We take the coffee and bagels back down to the lobby. Then we go back upstairs to spend the rest of the day making use of the bed.

Everything's perfect until it's time to get ready for the event, when Helen's mood goes into freefall.

Cranky, anxious, and way the hell too worried about her appearance, this is not the woman I've watched tell movie execs no without breaking a sweat. *This* Helen has changed outfits three or four times in the past twenty minutes. I thought she looked great in all of them, but she isn't happy.

"Jesus, woman. You could wear Daisy Dukes and a wifebeater and look awesome."

She shoots me a look that makes it clear I should clear out. "I'll be down in the lobby whenever you're ready."

Downstairs, I get some good meditation time in, despite all the activity in the lobby. I'm not excited about making small talk with a bunch of suits, but I am determined to get myself in a headspace where I can be a steady presence at her side while she faces whatever battle she's girding herself for. Helen may be all "I'm in control" on the outside, but there's a little girl in there somewhere who needs someone to hold onto. I may not be a hotshot like the people we'll be rubbing elbows with tonight, but I've been told I give a damn good hug.

When she eventually emerges from the bank of elevators, I just stand and open my arms wide. She rolls her eyes and grumbles something like "Don't mess up my hair," but she steps into my embrace. Once I've got her wrapped up, every jarring thing about this city is worth the trouble.

I'm the one who breaks the hug, but I immediately offer my elbow. "Shall we?"

She grunts an assent. "Let's get this show on the road."

Helen chose the hotel because it's only a short walk to the DGA theater, so even though she's in heels, we're there in minutes. Before we enter, she stiffens her spine and pastes a smile on her face.

When Ford and I would go to industry gatherings in LA, the glamour level was a hell of a lot lower than what we step into. It's obvious from the get-go that the DGA is operating in a whole different sphere than sound guys, who are really just a bunch of electronics geeks. There are, like, famous people here. Up-and-coming actors and actresses, directors and producers so well-known that anybody'd know who they were, even me. I about fall out when I see Steven Spielberg chatting to Ang Lee, but Helen seems unfazed by the celebrity fest, nodding and stopping to chat with one after another.

But when a large man steps away from a throng ahead of us and scans the room, she goes stock-still. The guy looks familiar, but I can't quite come up with his name.

"Arnold Feldstein," she mutters under her breath, so softly I can't quite tell how she feels about the guy. Could be anything from awe to rancor to… lust.

"The guy from Movomax? Wow." I mean, he's only one of the most famous producers in the world. "Do you know him?"

"Unfortunately" is what I think she says, and when the man sees her and begins to walk toward us, she takes a halting step back. Instinctively, I circle her waist.

She gives me a quick squeeze but steps away to accept a handshake from Feldstein, nodding and smiling like she's not freaking out. After she introduces me, he turns around to pull a young, very pregnant woman forward. I assume he's about to introduce his daughter but he calls her his wife. Helen's eyes widen briefly, but her pleasant smile doesn't falter.

He makes a few comments about the show we just wrapped. It's clear to me he's trying to get a rise out of her, but she doesn't bite.

"It was a challenge getting shut down for three weeks," she says in an even tone any politician would envy, "but the crew really pulled together in the end."

"I heard you're on the shortlist for line producer on a film my old buddy Jeb Whitman is producing." Arnie's gaze shifts from mild to predatory in a flash. "The one that's shooting in Chicago, something about a record store?"

Helen pales, her mask slipping.

"Shall I put in a good word for you?"

Going on instinct, I put my arm around her before she can answer. "I am so sorry, but Helen promised to introduce me to someone, and I see he's heading for the door. So nice to meet y'all."

As I steer her away her face leaches of color, so I scan the room to locate the least crowded of the open bars. "Let's get you something to drink."

When we get in line, however, she squeezes my hand. "Um, I'm going to go to the ladies'. I'll be right back."

"Do you want me to—"

The muscles of her jaw twitch as she shakes her head. "I'll be right back," she repeats, before she turns and walks away.

## HELEN

I barely make it to the stall, unsure what'll happen when I close the door behind me. Something needs to escape past my lips, but it could be vomit, tears, or a howl of pain.

I haven't eaten anything today except half a bagel, my appetite tamped down by anxiety. I always get nervous before work events, but I had a feeling something would happen tonight. I just didn't think it would be this.

The large, ornate bathroom seems empty, but I can't be sure, so I just lean on the stall door and try to catch my breath.

"You are not going to cry over that bastard," I grind out. "He doesn't fucking deserve it."

It's shock, I tell myself. Shock at seeing him in person after so many years, and shock at seeing him with such a young, innocent-looking, pregnant bride. I knew he'd married again, for at least the third time, but it's a whole other thing to see it up close and personal. The image of her standing there next to him with her wide smile and enormous belly has me collapsing onto the toilet and giving in to the grief, hands in fists and silently screaming into the void as tears stream down my carefully made-up face.

Eventually, I remember that I left Sully with very little explanation. I have a feeling if I stay in here too long, he'll come after me, so I dab at my face with some toilet paper and then move to the sinks to do more damage control.

As I'm removing makeup smears with a paper towel, two women enter the outer lounge. I can't quite hear what they're saying at first, but they're obviously arguing. I don't want them to think I'm eavesdropping, but before I can make a noise to let them know I'm in here, I hear his name. And more.

"Arnie fucking Feldstein."

"I just can't believe it. That poor girl. It makes me want to puke," the other woman says, her tone echoing my own feelings.

"Do you want to go? We can go."

"Let me just calm down a minute. I can't even think right now."

"I thought Arnie was in LA, I swear."

Without registering that my body has moved from the sinks to the outer lounge of the ladies' room, I say, "So did I."

Two heads whip around to face me. "Don't blame yourself. He hasn't been to a New York DGA event in years."

"Who are you?"

"Were you listening to us?"

"I'm sorry, I was"—my hand flails in the direction of the toilets—"I couldn't help but overhear."

"Great. This night just gets better and better. Are you from the *Hollywood Reporter* or something? Looking for a scoop?"

"No, no, I… I think I may have had a similar experience to —" My gaze ticks back and forth between the two women seated on the couch, trying to figure out which one was Arnie's likely victim. When the brunette takes the blonde's hand protectively, I get my answer. "To yours."

Figures. The pregnant girl outside is a blonde too.

Instead of surprise, the woman on the couch barks out a harsh laugh. "Well, welcome to the club."

Fifteen minutes later, I walk out of the lounge in a daze.

I never, ever thought about the possibility that there would be others. In a fucked-up way, I guess I thought I was special.

*You talk about this, you'll never work in this town again.*

The very words he'd used to threaten me, he'd used on that woman. And on dozens of others, according to her.

"He's not the only man in this business to use his position to feed his appetites," she'd said. "But he's particularly good at it. So good that you don't know what's happening until he's kicked you out on your ass."

Like me, she'd worked for him. Like me, she'd been singled out, mentored. In life as well as in the business. Everything from what to wear, to what fork to use.

Then, when he got bored, he ended it.

# CHAPTER 29

"It's not your fault. It's not your fault. It's not your fault."

—*Good Will Hunting*

## SULLY

I WAIT by the bar with two sweating drinks in my hands for a long time, afraid to move from this spot. When I can no longer stand it, I leave the drinks and go after her, searching every face in the seething crowd as I move through it, almost wishing I was still on crutches so people would get out of my way. Finally, I see her. Her color's back, but she still looks upset, and I fight my way through the throng until I've got her in my arms.

"Ready to get out of here?" I murmur into her ear.

When she nods into my chest, I put an arm around her shoulders and find the exit. I don't stop moving until we're back to our hotel. She doesn't say a word, and once we're in the room, she just turns and points to her back. After I unzip her dress, she steps out of it and her shoes, and crawls across the bed to lie on her side facing away from me.

"Do you… can I get you anything?"

She doesn't turn or speak, but reaches an arm behind her, fingers spread wide.

I shed my suit, strip down to my boxers, and slip on to the bed to cradle her while we breathe, together.

When I wake, I'm completely disoriented. I'm alone in an unfamiliar bed, but it's not until I register the faint glow of neon and streetlights outside the windows that I remember: New York, hotel room. I have a moment of panic when I realize that Helen should be next to me, but then the bathroom door clicks, and she creeps across the room.

"Hey."

"Did I wake you?" she whispers.

I lever up to look at the clock. "Four a.m. Ugh."

She's changed out of her sexy underwear and is wearing one of my T-shirts instead, which makes me inexplicably happy. She still looks hollowed-out, so I sit up and push the covers that we'd slept on top of down, and then hold them open for her. After she climbs in, she whispers, "I'm sorry."

"For what?"

"For all of it. Waking you up. Dragging you to this godawful city and then leaving the party after ten minutes. For"—her hand flaps in the air—"the drama."

"S'okay," I whisper into her hair. "You're a pain in the ass, but you're worth it."

We lie there for a few moments not saying anything, but I'm now wide awake, and her body is a bundle of tension, so I ask, "Do you want to talk about it?"

"I don't know. I'm afraid that you'll look at me differently."

"What? Like, how?

Her shoulders lift and fall in the tiniest of shrugs. "Like you'll lose respect for me."

"I honestly can't even imagine that. You are the most kickass woman—person—I know."

She just sighs in response, her breath hitching slightly on the exhale.

I pull her even closer, if that's possible, wanting her to feel what I'm saying as well as hear it. "If I've learned anything this past year, it's that how a person responds to challenges says a hell of a lot more about them than any accomplishments they might've racked up."

"Yeah, that's the thing." She shifts next to me, and I can just see her hands cupped over her face in the dim light. "Intellectually, I know that I'm not the person who should feel shame here. But I do. Because of how I handled it. And after what I learned tonight... I feel even worse."

I don't say anything, because whatever it is, it seems like she needs to be ready to tell me. So I wait.

"It happened when I was just starting out," she begins. "I'd wheedled my way into a job at Movomax, literally in the mail room."

The moment she says the name of that company, my stomach drops. Of course. It's about that guy.

"Arnie was this larger-than-life presence. He was also an asshole, but he was no scarier than my dad. I knew how to deal with guys like him. You make sure they don't notice you. If they do, you never show fear. For whatever reason, he noticed me. One day I was walking the halls, pushing a mail cart, the next I was working in his office. Filing, typing, answering phones."

It's hard to imagine this version of Helen. I mean, with her family situation she was probably tough, but she was still vulnerable.

Alone.

"At first, I thought he was taking a fatherly interest in me. He'd ask what I wanted to do in the business, we'd talk about how I could move up the ladder. He started giving me more responsibilities. But then, at some point, he started paying attention to me in a different way. By then I was working in acquisitions. He gushed over everything I brought him. All I wanted to do was please him."

The image of her *pleasing him* makes bile rise in the back of my throat, and I have to work to steady my breath.

"He started taking me to dinner and teaching me about fine wine and gourmet food. Even shopped for clothes for me. I was a poor kid from the wrong neighborhood even in Queens, so I ate it all up. Before I knew it, we were sleeping together."

She's been gesturing with one hand as she talked, eyes on the ceiling. But with this admission, the hand drops to cover her eyes. "Thing is, he was married. I *knew* he was married. I crossed that line, and I felt shitty about it, but he... dazzled me."

Her arm flops onto the sheet at her side, her head rocking back and forth. "It's no excuse, and I hated myself for doing it, but I couldn't say no to him. This went on for almost two years. Then, one day, out of the blue, he ended the affair *and* he fired me. I'd been at the company for several years by then. But the day I left, no one would look at me or talk to me. I lost everything."

She's not crying, but the pain in her voice slices through my heart, even as I'm practically shaking with the desire to find the guy and flatten him. "Helen, you have to know that he took advantage of you. He was older, your boss—"

And suddenly it's clear. Why she tried so hard not to let anything happen between us. "Oh."

"Exactly. And that's why I vowed that I'd never put anyone else in that position."

"But you don't have the same kind of power over me."

"And why is that? Because you're a man and I'm a woman." Her tone is so bitter, so sharp, I have to remind myself that her rancor isn't about me.

"No, that's not why. It's because I never wanted the job. Didn't really even need it."

"Seemed like you did when I hired you."

"It helped me get my shit turned around, that's for sure. But from what you've said, you were pursuing your dreams. To me, this work is a means to an end."

Her brow furrowed, her lips pressed together, she just stares at the ceiling, so I continue. "I love working on sets, but not because I want to be making TV and movies. I love how I get paid enough to *not* work for months at a time. My dream is to spend a chunk of every year on my boat, living simply."

I haven't said this to her before because I'm afraid it's not the kind of life she wants. Or thinks she wants. But it feels important to say it now.

"You do have power over me, Helen. In fact, I may be getting addicted to you. But not in the office. There, you're my boss, but you're replaceable."

"Gee, thanks a lot."

She's irritated, but I'll take that over despondent.

"As my *boss*, you're replaceable. As a person I love—" Her entire body tenses at the word, but I won't stop now. "As the woman I'm falling in love with, you're... it."

"And what is that?" she whispers.

"You're the only person I've ever known that can make me not care about anything other than making you laugh. Or moan in pleasure when I cook for you. Or cry out my name when you come."

I turn on my side, and then gently guide her chin with my forefinger until she's facing me. "I love you, Helen O'Neill."

Her chin trembles, and she pushes my hand away from it. Eyes bright, she says, "I haven't told you everything. So don't be too quick with those words."

The pain and self-recrimination in her eyes are killing me, but I don't look away from it. "It's okay, Helen."

She shakes her head. "I've never told anyone this. People

at Movomax knew about the affair at the time. But this, no one knows. Except him."

Again, I'm not going to press, but I'm not going anywhere either.

## HELEN

I don't know if it's Sully's soothing presence or the fact that I'm just so tired of carrying this shameful secret, but when he says, "I'm here," it pours out.

I tell him how I fell apart after Arnie kicked me out, how I cried for days. How I didn't want to live anymore.

Even as my heart pounds in fight-or-flight panic, I tell him how, sitting on the toilet, staring at my roommate's used tampons in the trash, I realized I hadn't bought or used such products myself for longer than I could remember.

How I raced to the Rite Aid down the street and bought a pregnancy test. How two lines appeared on the stick. How I read and re-read the instructions with shaking hands, willing the results to be wrong.

How I'd never wanted kids, hadn't wanted to be trapped like my mother was by me, but how my deranged brain latched onto the idea that being pregnant with his baby would make Arnie take me back.

How I showered and fixed my hair and put on makeup and Arnie's favorite dress. How I showed up at his office and demanded to see him.

How his face looked when I told him he was going to be a father. Not the light of joy I'd hoped for, but the sneer of disgust.

The cash he'd shoved at me.

The threat he'd uttered.

The one I heard echoed just this evening.

*You tell anyone, you'll never work in this industry again.*

How I took his blood money.

Made an appointment.

Took a cab to the clinic.

Got the abortion.

Took a cab back to the apartment.

And took a bus to California three days later.

To start over.

## SULLY

As Helen tells me her story in an emotionless monotone, I'm not ashamed to admit that my first impulse is to track that monster down and punch him in the face.

Over and over again.

It takes many deep breaths in and out to redirect that energy and just hold her until she stops talking. Still, I wait to make sure she's finished and I'm calm—or calmer—before I say anything.

"I wish I could make you feel better, Helen. I wish I could fix it. But all I can say is, this is not on you."

Her gaze doesn't move from the ceiling, from the spot she stared at the entire time she recited what happened to her.

"I 'took care of it,' Sully," she finally says, grinding the words out, her voice laced with self-loathing. "Just like he told me to. That's the kind of person you're with right now."

"You mean the kind of person who can move on from tragedy?"

"No, the kind that cares more about her career than being a single mom."

"Was it really a choice, though? He had you over a barrel."

"Still, I…"

After her words trail off and she just rocks her head from

side to side, jaw tight, I stroke gently up and down her arm, doing my best to soothe. "I know from experience that no one can talk you out of grief, and I can't imagine what your grief even looks like, but I want you to know that I don't judge your choice to not have the baby. Seems to me you took care of yourself and a potential life the best way you could."

"I don't want to be a victim," she says through gritted teeth.

"Then don't be." Pushing myself up to a seated position, I shift so my lips can reach the tears leaking down her cheeks. "Be a warrior," I whisper, punctuating my words with kisses. "Be a champion, be a protector, a defender."

"What if I don't know how?"

"Trust me. You do."

When she finally lets go, I'm there to catch her.

## HELEN

After I cry all over Sully, I slowly make love to him. He keeps asking if it's okay until the moment I drive him over the edge to a climax, but it's beyond okay. Not because I'm grateful to him, but because I need the connection. I need to feel the pleasure coursing through his body because I'm afraid if I don't, I won't be able to feel anything ever again.

We fall asleep in the wee hours of the morning, sleep too late, and have to rush around packing up in order to get to the airport to go home.

Him to Wallington.

Me to Los Angeles.

We spend the cab ride to the airport just holding hands. He's in a different terminal than me, but his flight leaves an hour later, so he shepherds me to my gate. Buys me a coffee and donut. Makes stupid jokes.

For that I'm grateful.

When it's time for me to board, he gives me a long, lingering kiss.

And then I panic.

"Wait. Sully. I don't know what this is. I don't know how to do this."

He just smiles. "Neither do I."

"But—isn't that a problem?"

He shrugs. "Do you really know how to do anything before you do it?"

And then he kisses me one more time and walks away, calling over his shoulder. "Call me when you get there."

"I will," I whisper, before making myself get on my plane.

# CHAPTER 30

"I wish I'd rung you. But then, you didn't ring me."

—*Four Weddings and a Funeral*

## SULLY

JUST WHEN I'M starting to wonder if I'm going to find a job anywhere in time to re-up my health insurance, Ford calls to see if I'm home and asks if he can come by.

By the time he arrives, I'm a little worried. "Everything okay?"

"Oh, yeah, totally," he says, accepting a greeting from Skye. "I just wanted to talk to you about this face-to-face."

"About what?" I ask as I sit on the couch, where Mr. Jones is curled up, completely ignoring the dog, who ignores him back. Lucy the dog trainer was in town over Thanksgiving and did her magic, so now the two live in peace.

Which has me wondering if the woman gives relationship advice too.

"I got a mixing job," Ford says as he settles into an armchair.

This has my attention snapping back to him. "Congratulations, man. That's great news."

When he doesn't light up like the Christmas tree blinking away in the corner, I add, "Um, it is good news, right? Isn't that what you want?"

He nods. "Yeah. And I was excited, but now I'm kind of freaking out. I have to buy all this equipment..."

His words trail off, and when he doesn't go on, I jump in. "But that's good in the long run, isn't it? You make money on renting it back to the studio."

"In theory," he says. "But I just started to worry about it all. Like, what if I fuck up and no one wants to hire me again?"

"Did you have any issues when you ran sound for second unit this fall?"

"No, but that was just a single day at a time. And it wasn't my own set up, I used the mixer's extra stuff."

"I hate to say it, Ford, but it sounds to me like you're looking to borrow trouble."

His gaze drops to his hands, which are clasped tight. "Maybe, but—I just wanted to ask... Would you consider coming with me, to boom on the job? It shoots in Santa Barbara, only a few hours' drive from LA. You could see Helen on the weekends."

I don't mention the fact that Helen might actually be in Chicago. I kind of owe my career—such as it is—to Ford, so I feel somewhat obligated to help him out, if I'd really be helping him. And that's the thing.

"Ford, I'm not sure you've really thought this through. I have very little actual booming experience."

"What are you talking about? You do it all the time."

"I get out there with the stick when there's a big crowd scene, but I don't know the things you do. About cutters and flags and feathering the boom. The finesse of it all. You'd have to be teaching me all that shit and figuring out your own job at the same time. Doesn't it make more sense to pick up some guy in LA who knows what he's doing already?"

Ford blows out a breath. "It does, but he wouldn't have my back like you would, Sully. I couldn't wig out and know you'd calm me down with your Zen self."

I snort. "Like I am right now?"

"Uh, yeah."

When Ford told me that his confidence wobbles, that he relies on me as much as I do him, I didn't really get it, but it's starting to make sense. "I wish I could help you, man, but if I'm honest, I'd rather take your place on *Lawson's Reach*."

"Why, is Helen going to run the show now?" His tone is bitter, but I'm not going to give him shit for it.

"She told me she wasn't interested. But I really need the hours. I have to do the safe thing for once. I can't lose my insurance right now. In fact, doing a short movie project with you would probably really fuck things up. I need work that lasts several months in a row to catch up."

Skye presses her nose into his clenched fists, until he pats her. "Yeah. You're probably right. About all of it."

"What? Has the almighty Ford Fischer admitted that Sullivan Calloway is right about something?"

"Puh. I think you have me mixed up with our bossy friend Violet."

Laughing, I chuck a pillow at him, and when he catches it, I get a glimpse of my buddy's smile. "How about this? We schedule a talk for a couple nights a week. Then you can unload about your worries to Buddha here, and I can ask you stupid questions about booming."

When he meets my gaze, I get the full-on Ford smile. "That sounds like a plan."

## HELEN

The first week after we leave New York, I talk to Sully every night. We don't talk about anything serious, just movies and music and food. The usual stuff. I get the sense that he doesn't want to bring up anything heavy over the phone, but I also wish he'd say something about what's really going on inside his head because my imagination is quite good at filling the void, suggesting everything from, *He's disgusted by you* to *He's going to get bored* to *How can you even be thinking about taking a job you don't want because of a man?*

Which is the thing I'm wrestling with at the moment.

Dani and Violet were right. *Lawson's Reach* is cleaning house. While shopping at Trader Joe's, I ran into the line producer on the show. We've known each other for years, and as we chatted in the snack aisle, I not only got an invite to his holiday party, but a tentative job offer. Basically, if he gets moved up to co-executive producer—which he thinks is ninety-five percent happening—and I want his old job, it's mine.

Of course, I never believe a job's for real until the ink's dry on the contract, but it's still got my panties in a twist. Literally and figuratively.

My body misses Sully so much I shorted out my vibrator.

At the same time, it scares the crap out of me to even contemplate making a choice because of a man. It's one thing if we try the long-distance thing and it doesn't work out. But it's a very different thing to move somewhere to be closer to him and it doesn't work out.

The problem is, the quiet sanctuary I've always loved returning to is a little too quiet. A *lot* too quiet. I meet friends for lunch or coffee or drinks, I go to holiday parties, but back at my place, I'm not only alone; I'm lonely.

My rental back in Wallington was a carriage house apartment with a random collection of secondhand furniture, beachy decor, and odds and ends obviously left behind by previous tenants. But by the end of the show, it felt more like a home than this tastefully decorated and nothing-ever-out-of-place condo ever has.

I not only miss that guy cooking for me and making me laugh and making me feel things I never thought I'd feel, but I miss the pitter-patter of Mr. Jones's little feet as he gallops through the apartment.

I could get a cat, but then what would I do with it when I go out of town? I don't have lifelong friends who'd take care of it like Sully does.

I've always celebrated my lack of strings, my stubborn independence, but I find myself longing not just for Sully, but for the backup he has. Yes, I've got friends. I make new ones on every show. But I don't have family or the kind of people in my corner that he does.

I get one call from an old fuck buddy who heard I was in town. I put him off with a lame excuse, but I don't say that I'm in a relationship.

Because I'm not sure I am. I don't know if I'm capable of sustaining one, even if we knew we'd be in the same place. The more I think about the agreement Glenda and her husband have, the more doing the long-distance thing worries me. I can't imagine just saying to Sully, "It's okay with me if you cheat," but I also know how tempting it can be when you're on the road.

Since he'd have any woman with two eyes in her head salivating with lust, I'd definitely have some competition.

When it comes down to it, I'm afraid. If I commit, not just out loud to Sully, but truly accept that I'm in love with that man, and then he backs out or gives up or moves on, I will be devastated. The wound will run much deeper than what happened with Arnie, even though I've only known Sully months and I was with him for years.

On top of all this, in regard to that bastard, my conscience has been picking at me since hearing the story of the woman in the bathroom. If I had said something back then, would I have prevented other women from being hurt? Or would Arnie have acted on his threat, ensuring that my career would be over?

I'll never know, and I don't even know if I have the power to make a difference now. I have a résumé, I've garnered respect for the way I've run productions, but his power has grown ten-fold, if not a hundred-fold. He built Movomax from a scrappy little company distributing foreign films to the behemoth credited with inventing the independent movie.

In a contest where it's his word against mine, he'd win hands down. Not because his story is more believable, but because he can make or break careers. The phrase "casting couch" wasn't invented out of whole cloth, and the movie business is as patriarchal as it was when I first got into it. Movies like *Thelma & Louise* are the exception rather than the rule.

Still, there might be a way to get the word out. A whisper network, where women could warn other women about predators like him.

Just as I'm turning possibilities over in my mind, my phone rings, and the name on the Caller ID has me picking up.

"Hey, stranger."

## SULLY

"Stranger?" I answer. "I've left you two voicemails since we talked last."

"I know, I'm sorry." It sounds like she's settling into some chair or couch or, I don't know, divan or chaise or something. I hate not being able to picture her because I know nothing about her life in LA. "I did call you back, but I feel weird leaving messages on the answering machine you share with Dani."

"She doesn't care."

"I care."

"Well, you shouldn't."

"Don't tell me what I should and shouldn't care about. You have no idea what it's like to be a woman. We get judged for wearing the wrong thing, being oversexed, being—"

"Hey, hey, what's going on? I get the sense this isn't really about Dani hearing a message where you say, 'This is Helen returning Sully's call.'"

"You're right," she says after a few beats. "I've just been stewing over what happened in New York."

I take a moment to get ahold of myself because I don't want my feelings for the man to leak into my words. "I get it, Helen. But I really wish you wouldn't give that asshole any more of your power."

A caustic laugh sounds in my ear. "Oh, he's got plenty of power without mine. That's the problem."

"Exactly. So why spend any more energy thinking about him?"

"Because he could still tank my career if he wanted to."

"I doubt that's true."

"Sully," she begins, my name laced with impatience. "You may have no idea what it's like to be a woman in the world in general, but you should at least know how this industry works. It is all about who you know. That's not just a meaningless saying. I can have a credit list a mile long, and he could still make a phone call saying that I'm 'difficult' and I'd lose the job."

It's shitty and she's right, so I really can't argue. And right now, she's like Mr. Jones when Skye would pin him in a corner, back up and spitting to seem bigger and stronger. But before I can figure out what to say to end the conversation so neither of us says something we'd regret, she continues.

"Like you and me. I'm a contact you should be capitalizing on. If you joined the DGA, you'd move up that ladder so fast. You have no idea how good you'd be, Sully. You're smarter than you think you are. You have so much potential."

Using that phrase with me is like waving a red flag at a bull, but I do my best to shove those feelings aside. "Helen. I told you I'm not doing that. Can you please drop it?"

"I just hate to see you waste the gifts you've been—"

"I'm already in IATSE, Helen. I'm not joining a different union and starting over." I'm not sure how successful I am at keeping the irritation out of my voice. I mean, how can she have spent the last two months with me and think I'd ever want to take advantage of our relationship like that?

"But you'd be a great UPM. Or first AD. You could be a director someday."

"Helen, I don't want to do any of those things. I liked my life the way it was."

"Before you met me?"

"Before the accident. I'd like that life, plus you."

"So I should just throw aside the career I've worked so hard to build over the past fifteen years so I can stay there and play house with you? On a damn boat?"

"That's not what I'm saying at all, Helen, and I think you know it. I'm just telling you what's important to me. Having health insurance is pretty important if I want to get back to one hundred percent. And frankly, if I can, I'd rather work here in town so I can be with my family and friends."

"Well, I'm afraid I can't arrange things so that I'll always be working in Wallington. With *your* family and *your* friends."

"But you could come here in between jobs," I argue, my mouth ignoring the message from my gut saying that I should end this conversation now. "Things would be easier if you weren't my boss. If we didn't have to worry so much about what other people think."

"But what about what *I* want? I don't want to settle anywhere, least of which in your bass-ackwards state. And if it's not evident from the shitty story I told you in New York, I don't want kids."

"W-who said I want kids?" I ask, wondering how the hell she made that leap.

"You're not even thirty. You'll start wanting kids right around when it's too late for me. Even if I wanted them, which I don't."

"I am really not sure how we got to kids and a picket fence here, Helen. It sounds to me like you're just spoilin' for a fight right now. Maybe we should—"

"It happens every damn day," she says, interrupting me. "It happened to Kara on *Hacked*. Women in this business, they get married, no plans to have kids. And then suddenly they've spit them out, and they hate it. Hate having no control over their lives anymore."

"So we won't have kids."

"That is not the point. You're not listening to me."

"No," I counter, struggling to stay calm. "You're not listening to me."

"You can't know what you're going to want ten years from now."

"Who can?"

"My eggs have an expiration date."

"So, if I want kids and you don't, we'd figure it out."

"Which would mean I give up on everything."

"Man, Helen. You couldn't be more of a fucking fatalist if you tried."

"Yeah, well, get used to it, Mr. Pollyanna. Maybe you should just cut your losses and bail out now."

"Congratulations, *boss*," I say, emphasizing the latter word. "You just got what you wanted."

The minute I hang up on Helen, I wish I hadn't, but frustration continues to roar in my ears long after I slam down the receiver.

The woman is stubborn and rigid and could start a damn argument in an empty house. And, like the dude in *My Fair Lady*, thinks she can make me over into an acceptable partner.

I'm sure she looked me up and down the day I stepped into her office and saw a guy who, like everything else in her path, she could fix. If he'd only listen to her and do what she said and get his shit together, he'd be worth something.

And all that talk about contacts and who you know? I can't do anything for her career. I'll never have the kind of power Arnie Feldstein wields.

Because I don't want it.

And if she can't accept me as I am, it is better to get out now.

I pace back and forth across my room, practically pulling my hair out. I can't run or swim or take my boat out, so I guess I'll have to take other measures to get away from the noise in my head.

Time to get drunk.

When I stumble out of my room later, passing the living room on my way to the head, I think my friends might be gathered on its couch and chairs. But that'd be silly. It's the middle of the night.

I think.

On my way back from the bathroom I stop to check, and it appears they're actually present. Not just in my imagination. "Wh-th-fuck-r y'all doin 'ere?"

Four heads turn in my direction.

"It's alive," Ford drawls.

Nate gives me a little salute. "Hey, Sull."

"Hi, Sully," Violet says.

"Nobody's answering my question," I say, doing my best to articulate all the sounds of the words, even as I note that I'm swaying on my feet. Which might have more to do with the alcohol in my veins than the lack of a cane.

Dani clears her throat. "Well, not sure if you remember this, but a couple hours ago when I came home, you were doing shots of Jack Daniels in the kitchen."

"S-So? Canna man drink when he wans to?" Damn. If I stop the swaying, my mouth don't work so good.

Nate appears with a chair and sets it down near me. "Want a seat, buddy?"

Pretending I could stand all night if I wanted to, I grab hold of the back of the chair and then drop my ass onto the seat. "Don' mind if I do."

But they're still staring at me. "What?"

"Well, Sully," Violet begins. "The last time you did shots of Jack Daniels was the day you quit going to classes at UNCW. So we thought, you know, something might be up."

"Puh. I'm fine."

"Also," Dani says. "You pointed at the phone and said that if Helen was to call, I should tell her that you'd moved to Wyoming."

"Wyoming? Why would I say that?"

Dani shrugs.

I'm confused for a few minutes, but then I remember. "Oh yeah. I'm mad at her."

"But it was the singing that had me calling everybody," Dani says.

"What singing?"

She looks like she smelled something bad enough to gag a maggot. "If you can call it that. At first I thought the cat was in a fight. But when I followed the sound, it was you, in your room, singing along with Patsy Cline."

"Patsy Cline?"

"Yep. And Alanis Morissette. And Celine Dion."

"But I hate Celine Dion."

She nods. "I know."

The caring expressions on my friends' faces do the opposite of helping me escape what happened. Instead, it hits me square in the chest, the pain slicing me in half. "I think I fucked up, y'all."

# CHAPTER 31

"One comes to a decision based on what one wants, not based on what one doesn't want."

—*Beautiful Girls*

## SULLY

THE NEXT MORNING, despite my friends doing their best to make me feel better about fucking things up with Helen, I'm not only hungover and sad, I'm confused.

"I mean, Sully, I don't want you to leave town again, but maybe you should move to California," were Dani's exact words when she found me still in bed at eleven o'clock this morning before she added, "Don't you have to be at the doctor?"

"Oh shit."

I arrive twenty minutes late for my appointment, but he's running late, so I don't get in for another half hour. At least I get some good news: while I need to continue therapy, I don't need to see the ortho for another three months because I'm healing right on schedule. He thinks by that appointment, he'll be able to sign off on surfing.

By the time I get out of there, I'm buoyed with hope but loopy from skipping breakfast and lunch, so I duck into my favorite sandwich shop on Front Street. On the way out, I must still be in a daze, because I walk smack into Whitney Moore.

Or, Whitney McRae, I guess. "Oh, man, I'm sorry, Whit, I wasn't looking where I was going. Are you okay?"

To be honest, I almost didn't recognize her. Whitney was always more put together than the rest of us, but now she looks like someone's mother.

"I'm fine, Sully." She extends her arm to examine the stained sleeve of her jacket. "Though my coat may have bought the farm."

I just stare at the greasy sandwich wrapper in my hand. "Oh, jeez. I'm such an idiot."

"Don't worry, I'm sure I can get it cleaned." She places a hand on my forearm but then quickly removes it. "I am glad I saw you, though. I really need to apologize."

"What? No, I'm the one who should apologize, Whit."

She shakes her head. "I heard you were in an accident. I'm sorry I never called, but I was all wrapped up in plans for"—a blush creeps up her cheeks—"you know, the wedding and all."

Biting back the words I'd like to say about her husband, I say instead, "I'm sorry I wasn't at the wedding."

"Well, it wasn't really your scene."

"Because I couldn't wear board shorts?"

She smiles, and for a moment I see the old Whitney in there. "Something like that."

We stand there kind of nodding and smiling for a few seconds. If I weren't so out of it, maybe I could figure out a way to ask if she's really okay. Or why she's dodging our calls. I can't seem to come up with the right words, but I do want to apologize before I lose the chance.

"Seriously, though, I'm sorry about what happened last

summer. I never should've put you on the spot like that. Or used you like that."

Her eyebrows come together briefly. "What do you mean?"

"I mean, that ultimatum. That was totally out of line. I do love you, Whit." An odd, panicked look crosses her face briefly, and I rush to clarify. "Like I love all y'all. Dani and Vi and Ford even. But what I said—I realized later, that was really more about me and Ford. I just wanted to be the chosen one for once."

Her lips form a thin line, but then the edges curl upward, carefully. "I understand."

"And, I don't know how to say this, but I hope it's not—I mean, I hope what I said, and the fight Ford and I had... I hope that's not the reason you got married."

"No, no, of course not. It was just time." Something like pain flashes across her face, but she glances down at her watch, so I can't be sure. "Speaking of time, I am late for an appointment. But it was good to see you."

She steps to the side the same time and direction that I do, and we end up doing a little dance on the sidewalk until she laughs, and I clear out of her way. I stare after her, and before she can turn the corner I call out, "Hey, Whitney?"

She turns and shields her eyes from the sun. "Yes?"

"Are you happy?"

She laughs lightly, shaking her head. "Of course. Hardy treats me like a princess. You know I can't resist that."

It occurs to me that while Violet was the one in our group that was the most devoted to theater, it's possible that Whitney's the best actress, though she's never stepped onstage or in front of a camera. "Okay, well, you need anything, you call, okay? Anytime. Promise?"

After a beat, she holds up the little finger on her right hand. "I swear. Pinky promise."

And then she disappears around the corner.

After Whitney walks away, I head over to the river, needing to at least see the water if I can't dive under it, float on it, feel that salt on my skin. Now that I have time, I've been doing workouts in a pool, but the doctor said I still can't risk being knocked off my board or even slammed by waves until spring.

I only shove the sandwich into my mouth because it's there, I'm so shook by the encounter with Whitney. I've wanted the chance to unburden myself, get off the hook for even being part of the reason why she'd shackle herself to that asshole. But while she said that had nothing to do with it, I don't believe her.

Worse, I get the feeling that something is so wrong that she's not even facing it.

As I stare across the Cape Fear, watching its currents swirl, it occurs to me that it's possible Helen's doing the same.

Or maybe I am.

There's got to be a reason why I've never pursued a relationship with anyone before, and why I'm resisting doing whatever I can to make things work with her. It's become clear over the past couple months that a lot of the choices I've made in my life have been reactive. In reaction to my parents, to my brother, to Ford, all I've done is prove that I'm not them.

I'm starting to figure out what it is, or who it is, that I want to be, but am I just doing the same with Helen? Refusing to consider a new career path or a return to LA just because she wants me to? I mean, if I were truly at peace, it wouldn't matter where I lived or what job I took. It'd only matter how I existed in the world, whether I live in North

Carolina or California, whether I'm a boom guy or a second AD.

I'm not quite there, but I'd sure like to be. Maybe my next step needs to take me in that direction.

# CHAPTER 32

"I love you. You...complete me. And I just had... ""

"Shut up. Just shut up. You had me at 'hello.' You had me at 'hello.'"

—*Jerry Maguire*

## HELEN

I SUPPOSE SULLY WAS RIGHT, in that he's not exactly a Zen master yet, because after he hangs up on me, he doesn't call back. I don't call him back, either, and not just because I don't want to leave a message that Dani will hear. It's killing me that I'm not sure how to fix things.

Or even if I should.

Because I still think I'm right. What we have may be special, but we're in different places in our careers and seem to want very different things from life. What's the use of continuing to spend time together and get closer when it's just going to end?

Problem is, the more time I spend alone, the less my arguments *feel* right. I thought I had everything under control, ticking off the boxes so I'd gradually work my way up the producer ladder. I make more money than I ever dreamed possible, and I've earned it.

Not by sleeping the way to the top, but by being the best I can be at my job.

But now, there's a hollow in my heart that must've been there all along. Like I threw a rug over a giant crack in my living room floor and then pretended it wasn't there. All while carefully avoiding it.

Am I going to lift that rug up and deal with what's underneath it?

Hell, no.

But I'm also not going to waste any more time apart from a guy that makes me happy. Even if it can't last.

"Time to suck it up, buttercup," I say out loud. "Make the call, even if you have no idea what to say, even if he's not ready to listen."

Just as I reach for the phone, it rings. *Danielle Goodwin* flashes on the Caller ID. Thinking she might be calling with bad news about Sully, I actually tuck my hands in my armpits, afraid of what she might say. But when the machine picks up, it's not her voice.

It's Sully's.

"Helen." The way he says my name is so rich with feeling, I can practically see it float through the air.

"What about this?" he continues. "I'll do whatever job you can get me on a set, as long as it's IATSE, even if it means a pay cut. As long as I get my health insurance."

This has me stopping in my tracks. If he's willing to make that sacrifice, then maybe it's okay if I do.

"But…"

At this word, my gut clenches. When he doesn't continue, I reach for the phone. Just as my finger touches the speaker button, he says, "I don't want to work as hard as you do. Or as much, maybe.

"See, I'm not like Ford. I don't need to be the boss or make my mark or win an Oscar or an Emmy. I need time away from everything."

*Including me?*

"From the busyness of the world. Like I told you that day on the beach. I'm okay with working hard—"

His words are cut off by the damn machine, which hangs up on him. Shoving my hands into my pockets this time, I wait.

"Hi. Me again," he says when the machine picks up again. "So anyway, when I originally went to California, it was on an impulse. Or three. The right impulse was that I needed to see more of the world before I settled here. And I gave it a good long try. Working there and other places around the country. But that was the thing. It was all work, work, work.

"I became just another go-getter, one of those people who've never seen a sky brighten over the channel as they drive over the bridge, down streets quiet as a church. To a beach where Nature holds you in the palm of her hand. The peace of it all only interrupted by the skitter of birds and the lap of waves at the shore." He sighs, but it's a sigh of pure contentment. "It's by far the best way to start the day."

*Better than next to a warm body? My body?*

Before he can continue, the machine hangs up on him, and I must hold my breath until he calls back because it rushes out of me when I hear his voice again.

"Hey. Me again. Where was I? Oh yeah. Of course, I'd like to also wake up next to your warm, sexy body. And wake you up with coffee and kisses when I return."

When he pauses, I almost pick up the receiver. He's making it very difficult to remember why I want to live all by myself in Los Angeles.

"If LA is where you need to be, I will do my best to make that work. If you're on location and there's a job for me, I'll do that. But here's my question. Could you work less? Like, take fewer jobs? So we can take part of the year to float?"

*Could I? But what would I do if I wasn't working?*

"Before you answer, I'm gonna tell you a story I heard on a tape today. A man's walking down the road, and he sees a man on a horse approach in the distance, riding hell for leather. When they get close enough, the man on foot calls, 'Sir! Where are you going so fast?'

"As he races by, the other man answers, 'I don't know! Ask the horse!'"

There's a pause before he continues. "Okay, I'll stop wearing out your answering machine tape. Call me, Helen. I miss you." He clears his throat. "Please don't shut me out. Or assume what I want. Talk to me, that's all I'm asking."

Once again, his voice is replaced by the ugly buzz of the dial tone.

I yell, "Who is the horse in that story?" at the infernal thing, but I don't have to be a Zen master to come up with the answer.

## SULLY

Helen still hasn't called me back.

It's making me crazy.

Especially since I have nothing else to do. I landed the *Lawson's Reach* job, but the show's winter hiatus just got extended for a week because the top-level shake-up apparently led to the throwing out of scripts, which means they need time to replace them.

It also means two more weeks of vacation for me. A vacation I neither want nor need for once. I'm so desperate for distraction that I actually sort through and clean all my boat supplies and my surf shed. When Helen still doesn't call, I start scrubbing Dani's house from top to bottom.

I've just pulled everything out of the freezer so it can

defrost and begun sponging off its racks when the phone rings. Dani's eating lunch, but she doesn't move to pick up the phone. Irritated, because everything irritates me these days, I whip off the dishwashing gloves and stomp theatrically to pluck the receiver from the wall.

"Hello?" I ask, my voice harsh even in my own ears.

"Sully?"

At the sound of Helen's voice, my heart skips a beat. "Hey, yeah. It's me."

"Oh. You sounded… funny."

"I was just… defrosting the freezer."

"Oh."

I hate the awkwardness between us, made even more uncomfortable by the presence of Dani at the kitchen table, but when I send a look her way, she pretends not to understand and just smiles sweetly.

Not wanting to let go even long enough to switch to the cordless phone, I walk into the hall, stretching the cord to its limit.

"Is, um, everything okay?"

"Yes, it is."

Her tone is business-like, making my mood plummet even further. Sagging onto the floor, sure that she's calling to break things off for good, I'm waffling between hanging up so she can't or telling her I'll join the DGA and let her turn me into a UPM if that's what she really wants, when I realize she's talking.

"… and you'd better take it too." When I don't answer because I'm embarrassed to say that I wasn't listening, she asks, "Are you still there? Sully?"

I clear my throat. "I'm here but, uh… something must've happened with the reception so I—oh, fuck it. I'm not going to lie to you. I was so worried about what you were going to say that I wasn't listening. So, um. What did you say?"

There's a long silence. "I said, after a lot of thought, I

decided to sign on with *Lawson's Reach*, so you better have too."

My heart's pounding so hard in my ears that I'm not sure I heard her right.

"Did you hear me this time?"

"Yes. Yes. I think so. But are you sure, Helen? I mean, did you get my messages? I mean, you're right, it shouldn't always be the woman giving stuff up because that really isn't fair, and I don't want to have you do that and then resent me, or even be unhappy. You being happy is what's—"

"Sully. I've taken the job. I took it because I wanted to. So get over yourself."

"Oh. Okay."

"I mean why would I want to be freezing my ass off in Chicago when I have my own personal chef in Wallington?"

"When you put it that way—"

"You know, I thought I'd arranged my life perfectly. But now I find there's a damn Sully-shaped hole in it. I hope you're prepared to fill that hole."

I can't help myself. I snort-laugh.

"For fuck's sake, Sully. You know what I mean."

This time a giggle flies out of my mouth. "I hope I know what you mean, cuz I miss that hole, if you know what I'm saying."

"I am going to hang up now. I will email you with my itinerary. Which includes finding us an apartment."

"Us?"

"Yes, us. You, me, and Mr. Jones."

My grin's so wide it hurts. "Got it, boss."

She doesn't say anything, but doesn't hang up either, and I don't want to be the first one, so I just curl up on the floor and wait.

"Love you, Calloway," she finally says.

"Love you too, O'Neill."

When we hang up, we do it together.

# CHAPTER 33

"The mind can go in a thousand directions, but on this beautiful path, I walk in peace."

—Thich Nhat Hanh

"I'm the king of the world!"

—*Titanic*

*FIVE MONTHS LATER*

## SULLY

When Helen emerges from the jetway, her spiky hair going in every direction, my heart does a little jig of joy at the sight of her. She scans the waiting crowd, and I raise a hand to wave, enjoying the freedom of having two solid legs beneath me. She returns the wave, but her smile's a little dim, so I rush to meet her.

"You okay?" I give her a quick hug and kiss before easing her bag off her shoulder.

"Yeah, just wiped out," she says over a yawn. Punching

me lightly, she adds, "I told you not to let me take the red-eye again."

I give her shoulders a squeeze before we begin walking toward the exit, just because I can. "Like I can tell you to do anything."

"Hmph," is her only answer.

"We're all packed up and ready to go."

She slows down when we pass the airport cafe. "Their coffee is crap but I need caffeine."

"I've got a thermos full of coffee with your name on it in the car, boss."

That earns me a kiss before she yawns again. "I better make a pit stop, though."

Ten minutes later, we're at the curb, loading her bags into Dani's car.

She had a busy week in LA, finding a tenant for her condo while working on postproduction for *Lawson's Reach*. "Are you sure you're okay with driving up to the boat today? We could wait until tomorrow."

"Actually, I can't," Dani says from the front seat. "I've got to work Monday, so I have to do it on the weekend."

"We could always rent a car."

Helen waves the idea down. "I'll be fine. I'll sleep in the back seat with the cat. Hello, Mr. Jones," she adds in a baby voice as she climbs into the car.

By the time I've closed her door and settled in my own seat, she's already greeted Dani, made a pillow out of a sweater, and snuggled up with the cat.

"She's exhausted," I mouth to Dani.

"Don't talk about me," Helen grumbles.

I just reach back and give both her and Mr. Jones a loving pat.

True to her word, she's out by the time we hit the interstate.

"Well, if we can't talk about Helen, then I can't give you shit about the blissful look on your face either, I guess." Dani shudders. "You people and your lovey-dovey eyes are too much."

It's on the tip of my tongue to say that she'll get it when she finds her person, but I don't want to be that guy, so I change the subject. "I appreciate you driving us."

Dani shrugs. "I'm always up for a road trip. And I'm going to stay with my cousin in Norlina on the way back. I haven't seen her in forever."

She's got an impressive number of cousins spread across the southeast, and since she usually avoids her family, it's nice to hear that she actually likes one of them.

Before I can ask her about that, she slides a look my way. "Are we going to talk about it or not?"

I shoot a quick took to the backseat, where cat and woman continue to snore away. "About what?"

"About Violet having a baby?" Dani rolls her eyes. "Like there's anything else to talk about."

"Oh, right." Violet and Nate shared the news last week at dinner, but since I don't live with Dani anymore, I haven't seen her since. "Yeah, that's pretty huge."

"Pretty huge? It's like, mind blowing. Beyond belief."

"For them, yeah."

"For all of us, dude. We'll never see them again."

"Gee, I hope that's not the case."

We're silent for a while. She's probably pondering the changes of the past year the way I am. Whitney married, Vi pregnant, and me of all people in a committed relationship.

Eventually, she asks about the plan for our trip, and I fill her in on the route from Deltaville, where my refurbished boat waits, back to Wallington.

"We'll spend a few weeks on the Chesapeake Bay, literally going where the wind takes us."

"Sounds nice."

"I hope so. The weather's supposed to be decent." The good thing about working on a TV show—at least on one like *Lawson's Reach* that got picked up for another season—is that you know the length of your hiatus. We wrapped in early May, and don't start back up again until July, so we've got a solid two months off.

"Then we'll make our way back down the intracoastal. We'll mostly have to motor, but it's got pretty scenery. What about you? Are you going to take a trip or anything?"

Dani also works on *Lawson's Reach,* but she's still got four or five gigs going at once. "Nah, I'm going to use the fact that you and Vi are cleared out to do some work on the house. Freshen up the paint. Might redo the master bath.

"And don't tell on me, but George and Tina are"—she makes air quotes—"renting rooms from me."

"But they're hardly ever in town."

"I know. It's perfect. If I have to keep the extra bedrooms open for them, then my mama can't move my younger brothers in with me, but since they're only in town once a month, I'll mostly have the place to myself."

"Won't you be lonely?"

She shakes her head. "I see people plenty. And Helen talked me into driving for the new producing director that's joining the show, so…"

When she doesn't go on, I glance over and can't quite believe what I'm seeing. "Are you blushing?"

She skitters a panicked look in my direction. "What? No."

"Yes, you are." I try to remember what Helen said about the producing director. "Wait—isn't he an actor? And was in a movie that shot here a couple of summers ago?"

She hesitates before answering. "Mm-hm."

"And you drove him then too, right?"

"Yup."

"You like him."

"I do not," she squawks. "I mean, anyone with a pulse would find him attractive, but he's been with some actress for years."

I let it go because it's got her all het up, but I'm definitely going to keep an eye on this situation.

By the time we get to Deltaville, Helen seems more human, and Mr. Jones is all cat—that is, he's had enough of the car. After we unload and say goodbye to Dani, we spend the rest of the afternoon getting settled on the boat. I make a simple dinner with fresh produce I brought along and fish we picked up on the way in, and we tuck in early.

I'll just add that making love by moonlight is as romantic as it sounds.

The next morning, I bring her coffee in bed and get everything ready so that we can get underway. Unfortunately, the third time I ask her to move so I can complete a task, she blows up.

"If I'm just going to be in the way, why did you ask me to join you on this trip?"

"Uh… because I want to spend time with you?" Since this doesn't seem to be the answer she wants, I add, "Just, you know, relax and enjoy the ride."

She crosses her arms over her chest and looks everywhere but at me. "I can't just be a… what do you call the decoration on the front of the boat?"

"A figurehead?"

She finally meets my confused gaze. "I can't relax when you're running around doing stuff. Plus, what if there's another accident and you hit your head? I need to know what to do."

I'm used to handling the boat on my own, but she's probably right. "That's a good point, but it'll take me some time to teach you everything, so we might not get very far today."

She shrugs. "Isn't the plan to go where the wind takes us?"

Nodding, because breaking down each task will also help us both be in the present moment, I grab a line from the cockpit storage. "Let's start with knots."

Taking a deep breath, I unfurl my plan for the morning and begin to take her through the process bit by bit. It takes over an hour to give her a tour of the deck and teach her how to run the engine and deal with the lines. But once we're underway, the relaxed expression on her face as the wind blows through her hair tells me it was worth it.

After I finish winching in the jib sheets, I give her a salute. "Good job securing the lines on deck."

She looks pointedly at the perfectly coiled ropes before narrowing her eyes at me. "Are you making fun of me?"

"I most certainly am not. A clean deck makes for safe sailing." I step behind the helm and release it from autopilot. "I appreciate you doing this, you know."

"Cleaning up the deck?"

"Coming on this trip with me."

"Are you kidding? I'm excited about it. I mean, I'll be honest, washing my hair with Joy dish detergent is not going to work. When I told my hairdresser about it, she—"

She starts to move across the cockpit just as we hit another boat's wake. Staggering to regain her balance on the rolling deck, she manages to grab hold of a stanchion to right herself before she falls on her ass.

"Hey. One hand for you, one hand for the boat. Always." My tone is stern, but here on the boat, I'm the captain.

"Right. I forgot."

The disruption has us off course slightly, luffing the main. "Can you take the helm while I adjust these sails?"

"The steering wheel?"

"The helm."

"Right. But isn't that the captain's job?"

"The captain's job is to chart the course and do whatever's necessary to get us there safely. Right now, the captain would like his first mate to take the helm."

I do my best to keep a straight face through this speech, but after she clicks her heels like she's Dorothy and salutes me with an "Aye, aye, sir" I'm snorting with laughter.

After taking the wheel, she listens carefully as I explain what I'm doing with the sails: moving the mainsheet traveler until the sail fills again and then locking it into place.

Once that's done, I talk her through using the telltales and the compass to balance both direction and speed.

Then I step away. "You're gonna be an old salt in no time."

She shoots me a look that'd make a lesser man turn tail and run. "Watch it, mister."

"Poor choice of words. Sea dog?"

"Are you kidding me right now?"

"Jolly tar?"

"I think you better quit while you're ahead."

"I think you're right. Point is, you'll be good at it before you know it."

"Sully, I'm good at everything I set my mind to."

"I believe you."

"But while I'm still working on it"—she pauses to tip her head—"I want you close. Unless you have something else you need to do."

I do a quick check to make sure everything's shipshape before sidling in behind her. "Right here okay?"

She sighs and leans back against my chest. "Just… hold on to me."

Dear reader, as you well know, I can follow orders when necessary, so I do as asked. I hold on tight.

Thank you for reading Sully and Helen's story!

Need more of this pair? I do have fun little scene to share with my VIPs, so if you'd like to join, you can do so at followkarengrey.com.

# ALSO BY KAREN GREY

*You Get What You Give* Carolina Classics #1

When a fiery redhead and the guy she thought was a one night stand turn out to be rivals, his family feud causes shockwaves bigger than the surf stirred up by the latest hurricane.
books2read.com/YGWYGKGrey

*What I'm Looking For* Boston Classics #1

*The course of true love never did run smooth,* but in this smart and sexy retro rom-com with a finance-nerd heroine and a drama-geek hero, returns on love can't be measured on the S&P 500.
books2read.com/WILFKGrey

*Forget About Me* Boston Classics #2

An underwear model, a best friend's little sister, and a dog who steals the show make for an unforgettable mix in this bittersweet romantic comedy. books2read.com/FAMKGrey

*Like It's 1999, a holiday novella*

Love 'em and Leave 'em Alice Kim and "Hot" Steve Lowell are perfect for each other. It'll only take them ten years to figure that out.
books2read.com/1999KGrey

*You Spin Me* Boston Classics #3

If two lonely people fall in love over late-night phone calls, will meeting face-to-face make them, or break them? In this heartfelt, slow-burn retro romcom, it may be the end of a decade, but it's the beginning of a love story. books2read.com/YSMKGrey

*Child of Mine* Boston Classics #4

A single mom gets a job offer she can't refuse but has to work side-by-side with the one-night stand that doesn't know he's a father. Of her daughter. books2read.com/COMKGrey

## ABOUT THE AUTHOR

KAREN GREY is a *USA Today* bestselling and award-winning author of vintage romantic comedies with smart heroines and hunky heroes. Drawing on a long career as a performer, her retro 80's and 90's romances are populated with characters working both on- and off-stage in theater, TV and film. When not reading or writing, she's lounging at the beach or hiking in the mountains. Or dreaming about both with an IPA in hand and a dog or a cat nearby.

To get the latest news, join her VIP club at followkarengrey.com.

*(Author photo: Kate Mejaski)*

For news, bonus material & a free book go to:
followkarengrey.com

facebook.com/karengreywriter
instagram.com/karengreywrites
goodreads.com/karen_grey
bookbub.com/profile/karen-grey

Made in the USA
Columbia, SC
18 January 2023